Nancy Donoval
2415 24 Ave. So.

rlovisell@Fulbrightweb.org

YEATS AND THE MASKS OF SYNTAX

Yeats and the Masks of Syntax

Joseph Adams

Columbia University Press
New York   1984

The Andrew W. Mellon Foundation, through a special grant, has assisted the Press in publishing this volume.
Copyright © Joseph Adams 1984

All rights reserved

Printed in Hong Kong

Library of Congress Cataloging in Publication Data
Adams, Joseph, 1940–
Yeats and the masks of syntax.
Bibliography: p.
Includes index.
1. Yeats, W. B. (William Butler), 1865–1939—Language—Grammar.   2. English language—Syntax.
I. Title.
PR5908.L33A32   1984   821'.8   83-20011
ISBN 0-231-04818-1

For Judy and Paul

Contents

Acknowledgements		viii
Introduction: the Syntactic Masks		1
1	The Noun Phrase and the Determiner	13
2	The Noun Phrase and the Modifier	27
3	The Relative Clause	42
4	Additive Structuring	56
5	The Grammar of Time in the Mask	72
Appendix: Sources of Examples from Yeats		83
Notes		87
Selected Bibliography		95
Glossary		106
Index		109

Acknowledgements

For their generous contributions of advice, insight and encouragement, I am deeply indebted to Robert Kirsner, Joseph Malone, Edward Said, Mihai Spariosu and John Unterecker. Each has helped in important ways to shape my thinking about the problems addressed in this study. To Edward Said I am especially indebted also for his guidance and advice at the crucial early stages of my investigation and for his unfailing interest in its subsequent progress.

The author and publishers wish to thank the following who have kindly given permission for the use of copyright material: the Macmillan Publishing Company, for the extracts from *The Variorum Edition of the Poems of W. B. Yeats* edited by Peter Allt and Russell K. Alspach, copyright 1912, 1916, 1918, 1919, 1924, 1928, 1933, 1934 by Macmillan Publishing Co., Inc., renewed 1940, 1944, 1946, 1947, 1952, 1956, 1961 by Bertha Georgie Yeats; copyright 1940 by Georgie Yeats, renewed 1968 by Bertha Georgie Yeats, Michael Butler Yeats and Anne Yeats; copyright 1957 by Macmillan Publishing Co., Inc.

Introduction:
the Syntactic Masks

The subject of this book is Yeats's syntax – in particular, certain anomalous structures that I call 'syntactic masks'. The syntactic masks occur in scattered places throughout Yeats's poems, as isolated words or phrases, or longer stretches of language. These structures exemplify aspects of modern writing that, though certainly not new, have only recently been fully recognised or focused on in the critical arena.[1] The syntactic masks exemplify, for one thing, a shift in the relation of subjectivity to language, with the subject seen as a textual product or construct rather than a full centre of consciousness expressing itself through language. Syntactic masks also exemplify the role of 'difference' in language – a more familiar notion, especially in linguistic theory. Both these aspects link the masks with a larger cultural and philosophical shift that continues to be played out in modern language, literature and thought. The masks, on a small scale, embody the shift that is also taking place in larger cultural phenomena. A term for this shift is needed and I have chosen 'antiplatonism', because it conveniently and accurately sums up the shift as a turning away from certain well-known positions.[2] One way of thinking of the syntactic masks is thus as part of this emerging antiplatonism, a diverse movement that persistently plays against the platonism dominant in both Yeats and modern culture. The masks – because they are constituted and operate according to the antiplatonic relation of subject to language and the antiplatonic principle of difference (as opposed to identity, or sameness) – become a measure of the penetration of antiplatonism into Yeats's language. One use of the present study, then, is as a demonstration of the existence of a modern antiplatonism, operationalized, so to speak, in describable antiplatonic features of language – namely, those found in Yeats's syntactic masks. While it provides evidence for this larger argument, the present study also attempts to refine understanding of the syntactic mask in itself. If this formation is so rich in implications, it is worth detailed analysis. The way will be clearer then for other studies to trace further the mask's implications for understanding Yeats, to see if other poets use syntactic masks, and to determine the place of the syntactic mask in modern literature generally.

This study attempts to show what sorts of elements in Yeats's poetry become syntactic masks, how the masks are constituted and how they operate. The method used for the basic task of describing the structures is borrowed from linguistics. Syntactic examples are isolated, gathered and analysed, with linguistic formalizations brought in to help describe their structure and operation.[3] Roughly speaking, the chapters are arranged according to the size of the elements analysed, going from smaller to larger. The first four chapters also show a progressive arrangement due to resemblances and structural relationships among the elements analysed. The fifth chapter, dealing with verbal tense, stands apart from this progression. Its analyses, since they relate syntactic operations to a certain view of time, should influence in retrospect the way all the earlier structures are viewed.

Unlike many linguistically based studies, this is not a study in stylistics. The purpose is not to describe or define Yeats's poetic style. Even less is the purpose to make 'the trip from language or style to the soul', as Spitzer would want stylistics to do.[4] There is no attempt made here to read Yeats's thinking, personality or emotional life in the forms of his language. These goals of stylistic analysis are essentially directed by the platonic view of language and meaning. The goal here, instead, is to analyse those formations in Yeats's syntax that seem not to fit the platonic view. Stylistics is platonic in seeing language as expressive. 'The artist', Spitzer writes, 'lends to an outward phenomenon of language an inner significance'.[5] For stylistics and the platonic view in general, language is thus a vehicle for meaning. It encloses meaning in a special way and thereby enables literature to convey an author's thoughts and feelings. In this model, the palpable forms of language carry an inner core of content – ultimately, the individual personality or subject – that is both their *raison d'être* and the force that shapes their outward, physical qualities.

With the development of linguistic stylistics, semiotics and structuralism, it was felt that more refined analytic tools, based on linguistics, would allow the codes of language and literature to be more completely revealed. But these methods kept the traditional model of language. An example can be seen in Jakobson's structuralist poetics and its formula: 'The poetic function projects the principle of equivalence from the axis of selection into the axis of combination'.[6] Jakobson's essential point is that in poetic language there is a parallelism or doubling (due to the principle of equivalence) of form and meaning within the syntagmatic flow of language (the axis of combination). Such things as rime, the rhythmic repetition of words, and patterned structures in syntax are seen as doubling or reinforcing the literal meaning of a passage. In a poem, the formal elements add another 'layer' to the meaning, thereby creating a larger and richer meaning. But language, in this model, is still a vehicle for extrinsic and extractable meanings. In Jakobson's version the meaning in question is just a multi-layered complex, with a literal component and a component arising from the parallel workings of the formal resources of language.

In the work of the post-structuralists, another position toward language and meaning was developed, an antiplatonic one.[7] This is the position that fits most closely with that of the present study. If the syntactic masks do have antiplatonic aspects, an antiplatonic theory will be more receptive to those aspects than one rooted in the opposing tradition. The aim of post-structuralist analysis has generally been to show language operating in a text and, in a sense, producing the text. The emphasis has not been on connecting the operations seen in a text to any entity (such as a global meaning) different in kind from those operations themselves. This analysis is particularly opposed to the platonic tradition's hierarchical model, which has a prior and essential meaning (or even a generating subject) determining the form of language. Instead of conceiving of meaning as extrinsic to the forms of language, or as more important than those forms, the antiplatonic view sees an interrelationship, or play, between forms and meanings *in* the text – or rather, a play between forms and meanings *as* the text. Meaning and form can be discriminated as they operate in and as the text, but neither one takes priority. It is as if the dominant meaning in one of Jakobson's multi-layered structures becomes unanchored and all the parts, both forms and meanings, are then free to combine and disperse.

Form and meaning in the syntactic masks exhibit precisely this kind of disarticulation and play. A mask most often appears as a syntactic ambiguity, but as one having little to do with enriching the global interpretation of the poem where it occurs. The important thing about the ambiguity of the syntactic mask is that it is more or less unresolvable, so much so that an oscillation is set up between its alternative possibilities. With neither syntactic form becoming fully possible, no final meaning can be assigned. Form and meaning thus become radically dislodged from one another. Moreover, made up as they are of competing alternative forms, the syntactic masks never become integrated as complete syntactic units. In fact, they violate the very rules that normally allow a decision to be made as to the identity of a syntactic unit.

The activity of the syntactic masks is most easily conceived as taking place within syntactic paradigms, a paradigm being a set of individual forms that can grammatically fill the same position in a given stretch of language. The members of a paradigm normally enjoy a mutually exclusive relation to one another: more than one member-form cannot simultaneously occur in the same position in a given environment. Thus, in an environment demanding either a noun or a pronoun, the form actually chosen cannot be both a noun and a pronoun. What takes place with the syntactic mask is a violation of this normal state of affairs: two mutually exclusive syntactic alternatives do somehow occur simultaneously in the same words. Syntactic masks thus become radically undecidable elements stuck into a normal flow of discourse. Because of their undecidability, they tend to stand out as something 'other', something fictional or not quite real. In effect, they masquerade as what they are not: real and meaningful units of syntax. For this reason, the term 'masks' seems appropriate. The emphasis of the term, however, is not so much on their covering over something more authentic than themselves. In so far as their own syntactic reality is concerned, the masks do not hide some other essence. Their only essence is as a kind of seeming.

An example that can stand for many is a certain use of the relative clause.[8] In normal usage, a restrictive relative clause is closely bound, grammatically and phonetically, to the preceding noun. A non-restrictive is not. The two kinds of clause constitute a paradigm; they stand in contrastive, differential relation to one another. In Yeats's poems, however, a great many relative clauses for various reasons are neither closely bound to the 'noun head' so as to make them restrictive, nor fully separated so as to make them non-restrictive. The following example is typical:[9]

(1) The wayward twilight companies
    Who sigh with mingled sorrow and content

The clause – 'Who sigh with mingled sorrow and content' – can be taken as helping to restrict the reference of 'companies'. But it also might be taken as adding some non-restrictive commentary, information we need not really have in order to determine which companies are being discussed. In this case, the ambiguity seems to arise from two factors: the lack of punctuation (a comma normally precedes a non-restrictive clause) and the positioning of the clause after a line-break. Actually, even a comma before the clause would not have fully eliminated the ambiguity. In any event, as it stands the clause appears neither restrictive nor non-restrictive. Or else it is both. Since no decision can be made between the two rival types, the clause defies our efforts to identify it completely. Nor does it even allow its alternate forms to emerge fully as completed units. Instead those forms alternate, each undercutting the other. They thus take on the instability characteristic of the syntactic mask. Each alternate reading tends to become a series of different moments of contrast with its opposite.

Another way the Yeatsian relative clause becomes a syntactic mask is through a peculiar use of the relative pronoun. According to their occurrence in restrictive or non-restrictive clauses, the relative pronouns fall into two main categories. The *wh-* pronouns (*who, whom, which, where*, etc.) can occur with either type of clause; *that* usually occurs only with restrictives. But in Yeats *that* is frequently found with non-restrictives, including non-restrictives following proper nouns and personal pronouns.[10]

(2) What cared Duke Ercole, *that* bid/ His mummers
(3) Lionel Johnson comes the first to mind/ *That* loved his learning better than mankind
(4) And that enquiring man John Synge comes next, *That* dying chose the living world for text
(5) Or so did Tom O'Roughley say *That* saw the surges running by
(6) And live like Solomon/ *That* Sheba led a dance
(7) the tragedy began/ With Homer *that* was a blind man
(8) And God-appointed Berkeley *that* proved all things a dream
(9) Cuchulain *that* fought night long with the foam
(10) You, *that* have not lived in thought but deed
(11) And what can I/ *That* am a wandering-witted fool
(12) And I, *that* count myself most prosperous
(13) If you, *that* have grown old

In these clauses, which we would expect to be non-restrictive, *that* lends a restrictive meaning because of its standard use in restrictive clauses. The effect is to de-emphasize the proper noun's or pronoun's normal independence and full identifiability. There is a feeling induced that the nouns and pronouns, to be known completely, must be supplemented by the relative clause. So the clauses take on characteristics of both types of relative. The ambiguity is particularly marked in examples like (7), (8) and (9), where there is no pause indicated before the clause, either by punctuation or a line-ending. And where the noun is one that is unquestionably known – 'Homer', 'Solomon', 'Berkeley', 'Cuchulain', etc. – the conflict between the defining and non-defining functions of the clause becomes acute, simply because the defining force of the clause is totally superfluous. In all these examples, then, the result in varying degrees is a syntactic mask, a structure with no single identity.

In so far as they achieve their partial identities, the alternating forms of the mask define each other differentially. Each possibility is what it is because it is not the other possibility, because it is *different from* the other possibility. And that other possibility is defined through its difference from the first – and so on. The linguistic axiom of Saussure, 'dans la langue il n'y a que des différences' (in language there are only differences), is apropos here, except that with the syntactic mask the difference is not between a present form in the text and the absent members of its paradigm (in the 'langue').[11] With the syntactic mask two or more members of the paradigm are actually in the text. Their mutual and differential definition of one another thus occurs in the text rather than behind the scenes. The difference between them, operating in the text, brings out whatever definition the two alternatives have. What Yeats's text practically succeeds in doing is to show us difference itself. The syntactic masks are simply locations in a text where the chief mechanism of language, difference, can become a focus of attention because the individual products of that mechanism tend continually to displace one another.

Can difference even be isolated and spoken of? It is clear that Saussure felt that difference itself was somehow at work in language, because in the passage just quoted he goes on to say: 'une différence suppose en général des termes positifs entre lesquels elle s'établit; mais dans la langue il n'y a que des différences *sans termes positifs*' (a difference generally implies positive terms between which it is set up; but in language there are only differences *without positive terms*). If

Introduction: the Syntactic Masks

there are only differences, then perhaps it is better to say that the differences themselves are the 'positive terms'. But what would a structure made of nothing but differences be like? Can such idiosyncratic things as differences even be organised in a structure? Gilles Deleuze (a philosopher often grouped with the post-structuralists) notes that an emphasis on difference implies its own special reading of the world. 'Considérons les deux formules', he writes: ' "seul ce qui se ressemble diffère", "seules les différences se ressemblent". Il s'agit de deux lectures du monde dans la mesure où l'une nous convie à penser la différence à partir d'une similitude ou d'une identité préalables, tandis que l'autre nous invite au contraire à penser la similitude et même l'identité comme le produit d'une disparité de fond'.[12] (Consider the two formulas: 'only what resembles differs', 'only differences resemble'. It's a question of two different readings of the world, in that the one asks us to think of difference from a pre-existing similitude or identity while the other asks us on the contrary to think of similitude and even identity as the product of a basic disparity.) The first formulation is within the platonic tradition, which emphasises the dominance of identity, resemblance and sameness. The second view, the antiplatonic one, attempts to see difference as the more radical principle. In an analysis of the syntactic masks, clearly the second view would be more likely to yield an accurate description.

In *Différence et répétition*, Deleuze presents a model of difference that is helpful in understanding how the masks operate. The model is doubly helpful because it also includes the role of the subject in differential structures, thus bringing together both the main antiplatonic aspects of the masks. Deleuze's analysis can be best understood if his final model, the 'complex system' of differences, is first broken down into simpler notions – beginning with that of a single 'pure' difference.

What is implied by the notion of a single, radical, pure difference? First of all, as we think of it, a single difference takes on successive 'moments'; it attempts to 'vibrate' between two poles. But obviously those poles are not fixed – otherwise they would become the positive terms that Saussure says we must do without. As a pure difference, the difference must somehow seize the opportunity for unilateral action, as opposed to remaining a mere bridging between positive poles. Consequently, the poles must be differences themselves. Or, more correctly, the 'first' pole is a difference which can be different only by becoming yet another difference, the 'second' pole. So there is a paradox: the pure difference is different from itself! And, differing from itself, it does not remain itself; it loses its identity. It propagates its moments into what Deleuze calls a series. But the items of the series are not copies of the first difference: they are differences in their own right, just as radically different from the first difference as that was from everything else.

It follows that there can be no such thing as a 'first' difference. The fiction of a first difference is impossible because the 'later' (or, more correctly, the 'other') items of the series are no less different than the 'earlier' items. The series is thus reversible. A closer examination will show it to be at least two series (just as the repeated alternatives of the syntactic mask seemed to form two series). It is not hard to imagine a pure difference as both continually spinning off other differences and continually returning to itself as well. It repeats itself as the pure difference it is, while *as* that series of repetitions, it also is in relation to the 'propagated' series. In other words, the unilateral, differentiating, 'vibration' of the ('first') difference produces two things: (1) a series of repetitions of that difference ($O, O', O'', \ldots$); and (2) a series of new differences that derive from the instances or 'beats' making up the first series ($a, b, c, \ldots$). The two series necessarily correlate, but do so by virtue of their differing from one another. To describe the world of pure, structural difference, Deleuze uses the notion of series as shorthand for what must exist in place of unified, self-identical elements. But the concept of the series also helps clarify the properties of structures of differences. In the classic example from the structure of language, two correlative series are formed by the signifier and the signified. Each of the two series is differential within itself and displaced in relation to the other, so that at no point does an integral 'unit' of signified correspond isomorphically with a 'unit' of signifier.

The formation of series can be imagined as if some original, generative power lay in the pure difference, which then goes on to propagate itself into series. But it becomes apparent that the only way for there to *be* a pure difference is for it to be part of a series. A pure difference cannot exist except as a repetition. (Were it to come to a stop, it would fall into sameness and become identical to itself.) So, just as a pure difference must propagate or repeat, the series it belongs to must *differentiate*. But what has to take place for there to be a series with each succeeding unit emphatically *different* in and of itself? What must take place for the series to be a repetition of differences and not of samenesses?

Deleuze's answer to these questions begins with the notion of an ordinary series, a series made up of ostensibly *identical* units. In a regular succession of like objects (for example, identical soundings of a musical note), there is nothing that could properly be called a repetition (let alone a repetition of differences). Isolated items simply appear and then vanish. However, if there is some way of keeping track of the past items (memory, for example), then a series suddenly appears, and it becomes repetitious. If the past items are gathered, contracted, or conserved, then each new item can appear as an addition to, or a modification of, the contents already gathered.

Here, the notion of a subject becomes crucial. The necessary contracting or comparing agent can be nothing other than a mind or a subject.[13] In order for the simple, physical repetition to exist, there must be effected a change or difference in the past events. The subject is the agent of that change. The subject creates a contraction or tension among the elements so as to orient them toward the new item to be added. The tension or contraction sensitises the reservoir of past items and enables it to register the new item as belonging to the succession. But the *contraction itself* is also a difference: it is something continually differing from the set of individual items that have occurred. And this difference can be seen as the repeated difference needed in a system where the repetition must *not* be of identical items.

Each different contraction or arrangement constitutes an element in another series, a series of differences *withdrawn from* the original series. In a structure of two series, the repeated contractions naturally contract the differences of the other series, so the series always incorporate each other. Each difference encloses, contracts, or arranges a different grouping of items. Consequently, what can now be thought of as repeating is really the differing whole rather than (or in addition to) the individual item. The differing contraction is now no longer simply the operation that defines the original, elementary repetition; it is now what makes possible a total repetition of the whole series. The repeating whole is always different.

At this point, Deleuze's model finds difference and repetition to be absolutely correlative: the difference determines the repetitions, and the total repetition is of differences. Repetition in its essence *is* difference, just as difference in itself can only be between two repetitions. As for the status of the subject, it has now changed radically. As the system has become complex, the subject has not only become enclosed in it; but has ceased being the dominant agent, even ceased being the passive 'accumulator' for the simple series. Now, it is as if the contracting and differentiating are done *for* the subject, but subjectivity nevertheless 'attends' the differences wherever they occur. Subjects 'people the system', as Deleuze puts it. But they are shifting, local, fragmentary, momentary selves. Deleuze indicates their partial and incipient nature by calling them 'sujets larvaires', larval subjects. They perhaps underlie or build up to the more global entities traditionally called subjects. But within the given system, these 'small' subjects are the only subjectivities that can be said to exist.

Deleuze's model suggests the essential processes and dimensions of the syntactic mask. A syntactic mask is, in fact, a system made up of differential series. Each of the alternative forms in the mask is constituted as a differential repetition of the other form. It is a series of differences that resonates with the other series and repeats the other as they interact differentially with each other. The mask becomes no single form but a set of series propagated 'to infinity'. In a sense, it is the clash or resonance of the series that we experience in reading the mask rather than a single form with a single meaning. Deleuze's analysis brings out also the antiplatonic nature of these structures. The platonic view of language sees an individual member of a paradigm essentially copying or embodying a pre-existing pattern. The abstract, empty pattern – the paradigm – has an existence logically prior to the actual examples filling it. In the antiplatonic analysis, however, a differential system – such as language, or a part of language like the syntactic mask – paradoxically both does and does not pre-exist its embodiment. The series that we read as, say, the restrictive relative clause has its present identity only because of the contrasting series read as the non-restrictive. But the latter cannot be said to pre-exist the former because it needs to contrast with the restrictive's series. Embodiments and paradigmatic patterns are thus entwined and co-realised in the same system.

Syntactic masks confirm, too, Deleuze's antiplatonic view of the subject in language, showing it as something momentary and fragmented. The platonic view would have a unified and controlling subject as the source of a given utterance (such as a poem). But the masks reverse this position. The masks produce effects of subjectivity at scattered spots in the text. Wherever a mask structure appears, there is felt the momentary intensity of a subjective attitude. Frequently the analysis of a mask will show that a particular element (for example, a certain kind of adjective, or the 'distancing' demonstrative *that*) colours or characterises the subjectivity produced. But even lacking such characterisation, the masks always produce a certain partial sense of subjectivity. Deleuze would explain it as the memory-like function needed to effect or at least 'attend' the gatherings of difference that constitute the repetitive series. He notes also that in a complex system, the subject cannot be thought of as a unified, controlling cause because of the system's very complexity, with its many co-existing series.

So the syntactic mask as a producer of subjectivity reverses the platonic view of the subject as producer of language. This reversal is also found in Yeats's own theory of the self, particularly as it was worked out in *A Vision*. For Yeats, the development of the subject as an individual is the work of a complex process. The process involves Yeats's concept of 'the Mask', one of the paired elements whirling in the system of gyres. The subject begins to find its individuality when it pursues a Mask contrary to its 'true' self, a Mask with the likeness and character of its opposite spirit, its Daimon. But the subject is not truly an independent agent in this process. As Yeats writes: 'I am in the place where the Daimon is, but I do not think he is with me until I begin to make a new personality . . . and yet . . . not knowing when I am the finger, when the clay'.[14] In Yeats's model as in Deleuze's, the subject is never completely separate from the primordial field of tensions defining it ('My instructors identify consciousness with conflict', *A Vision*, 214.) The subject, the individual consciousness, is finally only a result within the system of gyres. It only comes about through the systematic play of oppositions, reciprocities and interdependencies among the 'Four Principles' and the 'Four Faculties' (including the Mask).[15]

If Yeats's theory is antiplatonic, so too are many others in the development of a modernist 'impersonal' aesthetic out of its seeming opposite, romanticism. Romanticism, in its idealist beginnings, separated art from contingent reality. But the more it defined art as a self-enclosed, autotelic realm (as the German idealists and Coleridge, following them, tended to define it), the more art began to fall back on its own formal resources and literature on the formal resources within language.[16] As that happened, the distance was widened and the causal linkage weakened between the word and the subject. In the literature of modernism, this distance often becomes a tendency to find the authorial subject either absent from the text (Eliot's 'impersonality') or a function of the text (Joyce, Proust).[17]

Another aspect of modern literature's antiplatonic 'impersonality' was the interest taken in the mask as a figure of artistic truth.[18] Writers such as Wilde, Nietzsche and Yeats himself invariably focussed on the importance of artifice or fiction as the means of achieving a higher truth – higher, that is, than the truth of straightforward, unmasked self-revelation. Wilde wrote: 'Man is least himself when he talks in his own person. Give him a mask and he will tell you the truth'.[19] Implied in the notion of the mask, however, is not just that the truth of the subject cannot be directly communicated, but also that the subject may not actually exist as a separate, unitary centre of consciousness. In other words, there is often the implication that the unitary subject can appear *only* as a fiction, a made object, an artificial construct.

The same view is implied in the modern analysis of language. The breaking up of language into sets of discrete objects for various kinds of analytic operations tended to take from language its referential power – or rather made that power usable only through indirect means.[20] Since language was a system of elements ruled primarily by formal, grammatical demands, it no longer enjoyed the immediate resemblance to things in the world that had formerly allowed it to refer directly to those things. A parallel change took place in the use of language to 'mean' the speaking subject. The subject also became subordinated to grammatical demands. In the model fostered by this formalised language, the subject became less a force capable of fully 'saying itself' and more a mere result of language, arising from the deployment of certain structural indicators.[21] A parallel to this condition of the subject is seen in the syntactic masks. But, instead of indicating subjects by means of the pre-existing, conventional markers of ordinary language (such elements as the pronoun *I*), the syntactic masks form their own idiosyncratic systems that evoke subjects through differential play.

The background of the syntactic masks, then, is the many-sided shift of modern culture toward the 'dispersed' and 'constructed' subject. As a modest contribution to understanding this movement, the present study offers an analysis and description of one small part of it.

1 The Noun Phrase and the Determiner

This chapter will consider certain syntactic masks created in the noun phrase by the behaviour of the determiner.[1] Determiners, including the articles, have as their general function the task of limiting the reference of the noun that follows. The different determiners have their various specific uses, but all of them also serve to indicate the degree to which the following noun is supposed to be identified or known to the hearer or 'allocutor'.[2] A determiner is a kind of pointer – it points either to a source of identification for its noun or to the fact that identification is lacking. The different modes of achieving identification thrust the determiner and other parts of the noun phrase into various sorts of relations – with other parts of the text, with presupposed information, etc. Conflicts between equally compelling modes of identification bring their differences into play in the text and create syntactic masks in the noun phrase. The conflicts are possible in the first place because of the variety of uses of the determiners, particularly of the 'definite determiners'.

The *definite determiners* indicate that the noun is somehow fully identified. A valid generalisation is achieved by including as definite determiners – along with the article *the* – the demonstratives and the possessive pronouns.[3] The demonstratives (*this, these, that, those*), unlike *the* or the possessives, have separate forms to go with singular and plural nouns – as do the *indefinite determiners*.

To say that a noun phrase is indefinite simply means that further identification is required for us to know exactly which member or members of a class are being referred to. The function of the indefinite determiners, singular or plural, is to signal that this needed identification has not been completely made. The indefinite article *a* only occurs with singular nouns, being historically a reduced form of *one*. Plural nouns have the indefinite determiner in an alogistic or 'null' form. That is, when plural nouns have no apparent article they are interpreted as indefinite, as in '*Banners* choke the sky'.[4] This significant absence of a word is referred to as the null determiner or simply as 'null'. Plural nouns with 'null' frequently indicate all the members of a class, as in '*Men* dance on deathless feet'. By giving a noun the most general sense possible, this use almost allows an indefinite plural noun to escape the need for identification.

The definite determiners show the claim of complete identification in various ways. The possessive pronouns show that the entity named is identified because it belongs to someone or something previously mentioned. *The* and the demonstratives have other ways of effecting identification. They both can refer us back to a previous occurrence of the noun in the discourse. The process of 'referring back' is analogous to the way possessives operate but here the identification is made because a previous occurrence of the noun itself provides the knowledge that allows the identifying link to be made. In both cases, the identification takes place through *anaphora* ('referring' or 'carrying back'). In Yeats's poem 'Symbols', for example, the noun phrase '*the* sword-blade' is identified by reference back to a previous occurrence: 'All-destroying sword-blade still/ Carried by the wandering fool'. Or, for an example with the demonstrative:

(1) I rage at my own image . . .
     . . . be warned and go
     If you have seen *that* image

The definite determiners, as M. A. K. Halliday notes, also may refer not to the discourse but to the situation – the physical setting – within which the discourse takes place.[5] That is, they identify a noun by calling attention to the actual, physical presence of the entity named by the noun. For example:

(2) I walk through *the* long schoolroom questioning
(3) In pity for man's darkening thought
     He walked *that* room[6]

This mode of identification can be called the *situational* use. In their situational uses, *the* and the demonstratives operate differently. The situational use of the demonstratives typically takes place (perhaps accompanied by the speaker's pointing) when an item must be singled out to distinguish it from other similar items or to mark it as a

The Noun Phrase and the Determiner 15

salient factor in the situation. The situational use of a demonstrative is to 'discover' a factor in a setting and introduce it into the discourse as something 'new'. The situational demonstrative does not refer to something already known or 'given', but rather functions to *create* the new knowledge necessary for identification. *The*, on the other hand, is used when the referent does not need to be singled out or emphasised, usually because there is only one of its kind present. But, to say, for example, 'the tower' when there may be several towers in view will not identify the one meant (unless it has been previously mentioned and *the* refers anaphorically to that mention). For *the* to function in situational use, the existence and identity of the referent must be a presupposed fact, a 'given' of the discourse situation. With its reliance on something presupposed as the ultimate source of identification for its noun, *the* functions more or less anaphorically in its situational use as well as in its properly anaphoric use. In each case, *the* points 'back' to pre-established knowledge to identify its noun. Generally speaking, then, in their anaphoric and situational uses, *the* and the demonstratives rely on the following sources for establishing identification:

	Anaphoric	*Situational*
the:	presupposed knowledge	presupposed knowledge
that, those, etc.:	presupposed knowledge	new knowledge

MASKS OF IDENTIFICATION

The fact that the same word can have different identifying functions opens the door for the differential play that will produce masks in these determiners and their noun phrases. What occurs in Yeats is that a determiner ostensibly functioning situationally will often have the anaphoric mode come into play, and vice versa. The two modes – or the two roles for the determiner – are thus thrust into competition and differentiation. The single determiner becomes split in two. Or rather, it participates in two mutually differentiating series. It becomes two competing but mutually defining members of the same paradigm, the paradigm containing the possible identification markers for that particular noun phrase. The entire noun phrase (that is, the noun as well as the determiner) seems to participate in this process, no doubt because the identification of the whole phrase is at stake.

Situational Determiners

In example (2) – 'I walk through *the* long schoolroom questioning – the ostensible mode of identification is situational. With the *the* placed near the beginning of the discourse, there is no textual antecedent so anaphora seems to be ruled out. Moreover, if the title of the poem, 'Among School Children', is taken into account, a potentially identifying context for the speaker's claim appears: he is apparently somewhere school children are found. But which schoolroom *exactly* is it? In fact, we do not know. The schoolroom's identity is completely vague, even though the noun is marked as definite and fully identified by its determiner. The presence of *the* makes the claim that the noun is fully identified, yet it clearly is not. But, with no clear situational source of identification, *the* has the effect of implying that the identity of the noun is already known to or presupposed by both the narrator of the poem and the reader. This implication, a strictly fictional presupposition, calls into play the anaphoric mode of identification – not because there is any actual antecedent, but only as a result of the unexplained presupposition. If the schoolroom is supposed to be known to us, then the illusion of a prior mention comes into play. The reader partly feels that, somewhere, a discourse has mentioned the 'long schoolroom' and hence the present mention is justifiably definite. But the presupposed knowledge simply does not exist as such. As a result, the anaphoric mode remains in an uneasy competition with the situational mode (which continually slips back into play). The consequence is a syntactic mask, and the same kind of process takes place with all the masks using situational determiners.

Masks using *the* 'situationally' are very common in Yeats. These are just a few of many possible examples:

(4) The brawling of a sparrow in *the* eaves
(5) I stumbled blind/Among *the* stones and thorn-trees
(6) *The* cataract smokes upon *the* mountain side,/ . . . /
(7) *the* sea-wind . . . upon *the* tower,
     And under the arches of *the* bridge

(8) I met the Bishop on *the* road
(9) *The* curtains drawn upon unfriendly night
(10) Bolt and bar *the* shutter
(11) Quiet *the* dog, tether *the* pony

In each case, the definite identity of a noun phrase is indicated as resting on the implied existence of a known situation. But without the actual existence of such a situation shared between locutor and allocutor, the situational use of *the* continually yields to another source of identification for the noun, the anaphoric, with its strong presuppositional force. That, however, yields in turn, and the process of the mask continues.

The subjectivity of these masks seems to come about as one mode of identification slips over into the opposing mode. As semantic components of the syntactic forms, the two competing 'locations' of the presupposed knowledge – the situation and a presupposed mention of some sort – also form resonating series of differences. As one location subverts the other, what seems to remain, and even come to the foreground, is just the quality of there being a presupposition at work. It seems likely that whatever subjective qualities exist in a mask's components (such as presupposition) become focussed and intensified by the action of contracting and gathering that takes place in the series. We thus experience particular moments of subjectivity as we read phrases like 'the eaves' in (4) or 'The cataract' in (6), sensing the oscillating movement between different modes of identification.

In Yeats, the presuppositional component of this type of mask can be especially noticed when the masks occur in certain meditative poems (example (2) is from one of these poems). The very issue of identification is brought to the fore in these cases, probably because the situation is established through a conventional fiction: a dramatic monologue of sorts is often set up, with the Yeatsian 'I' meditating within a specified physical setting.[7]

(12) I pace upon *the* battlements and stare
(13) *The* trees are in their autumn beauty
(14) *the* water/Mirrors a still sky
(15) As at *the* loophole there/*The* daws chatter
(16) *The* bees build in the crevices/Of loosening masonry
(17) I climb to *the* tower-top

(18) I turn away and shut *the* door, and on *the* stair
(19) two long glasses brimmed with muscatel/Bubble upon *the* table
(20) Under my window-ledge *the* waters race
(21) Here at right of *the* entrance this bronze head

In examples like these, with the situation fictionalised, the presupposition due to *the* induces the other possible mode of identification, the anaphoric – and the two modes are thrust into competition.

A similar thing happens when the situational *demonstratives* are used. These forms occur, for example, in 'The Phases of the Moon':

(22) *that* shadow is the tower
(23) He has . . . chosen *this* place to live in

And in 'Michael Robartes and the Dancer':

(24) In *this* altar-piece the knight,
Who grips his long spear so to push
That dragon

And again in the following lines from other poems:

(25) *This* night has been so strange
(26) Beyond *that* ridge lived Mrs. French
(27) How can I, *that* girl standing there,
My attention fix

The presence of the object (or person) that justifies the definite determiner is perhaps simulated by a kind of dramatic illusion in these cases. But the claim of identification by virtue of the situation fails, just as it did in examples (12)–(21) and for similar reasons.

The masks created in these cases again involve the difference between the situational and the anaphoric modes of identification. They are also constituted by another contrast – the contrast between the attempts to use new knowledge (the situational mode) and presupposed knowledge (the anaphoric mode). In (26), for example, the new information supposedly created by the demonstrative in its situational use might be something like: 'a ridge somewhere in the vicinity is to be taken note of, and the ridge to be noted is the specific one now being indicated (somehow) by the speaker'. But this information seems to be continually displaced by the sense that the speaker has previously mentioned 'that ridge'.

In some cases, the situational demonstratives seem to carry off the dramatic illusion, obscuring the fact that the forms are syntactic masks. In 'To be carved on a stone at Thoor Ballylee' the dramatic illusion and the situational mode seem to win out:

(28) I, the poet William Yeats . . .
Restored *this* tower for my wife George;
And may *these* characters remain

Here situational demonstratives help create the illusion that the written discourse itself, the poem (in the form of an inscription) is, or will be, close enough to its referents to justify the situational use of the demonstratives. The supposed proximity of the referents to the locutor (here, the inscription) is indicated by the choice of *this* and *these*. The illusion would clearly fail if *that* and *those* were used, for then a distance would be created between the putative speaker and the referents justifying the situational use.

Anaphoric Determiners

Syntactic masks come about with anaphoric determiners by the same process that takes place with the situational determiners, except with some reversing of roles. Here, it is the anaphoric use that is set up by the ostensible demands of the text. That use then comes into conflict and differential competition with certain aspects associated with the *situational* use.

These masks tend to appear more frequently with the demonstrative than with *the*. The apparent reason is that ambiguous uses of *the* seem to be more readily interpreted as situational uses rather than as 'faulty' anaphoric uses. The two uses of *the* are actually closer than the corresponding uses of the demonstratives, since with *the* both uses employ presupposed knowledge. Consequently, it is often a matter of choice as to whether an ambiguous example is categorised as situational or anaphoric. The italicised noun phrase in the following example might be either anaphoric or situational.

(29) A shadow of cloud on the stream
Changes minute by minute;
A horse-hoof slides on *the brim*

Here 'the brim' might be identified simply because the noun phrase 'the stream' textually supplies a sufficient antecedent for an anaphoric reference. Or else, if the situational illusion is felt strongly enough, the supposed presence of a stream would provide the situational context for identifying a whole class of related nouns, including 'brim'. Again, in 'Cuchulain's Fight with the Sea', after a reference to 'Emer, raddling raiment in her dun', the following line occurs:

(30)   Then Emer cast the web upon *the floor*

The identification here is made by reference to the earlier setting – either anaphorically or situationally. In either case, the activity of the mask is not affected.

Whatever may be the case with *the*, there are clear instances in Yeats where *demonstratives* are used anaphorically and then result in masks. As the term is broadly applied in this study, anaphoric identification, though depending essentially on reference back to a presupposed fact, need not make use of a textual antecedent. The essential requirement is just that there be a presupposition that the identifying fact is known. In Yeats, anaphoric demonstratives are frequently used without textual antecedents, and as a result an emphasis is placed on the needed presupposition. An example can be seen in the following lines which begin 'A Deep-sworn Vow':

(31)   Others because you did not keep
        That deep-sworn vow have been friends of mine

The noun 'vow' is not identified situationally – it does not single out an element in a physical situation – nor is there a previous textual mention. The poem's title stands outside the discourse, and in any event would not suffice as identification, having no defining context of its own. The modifier 'deep-sworn' does not identify the 'vow' either, although it describes it. Clearly the noun phrase must be taken as referring back to something presumed known to both the 'I' and the 'you' mentioned in the poem, a fact presupposed by the speaker to be known to his hearer. The existence and identity of the vow are the presuppositions of the discourse that the determiner refers to anaphorically.

The strong emphasis given to presupposition in (31) is a characteristic effect of the anaphoric demonstratives when there is no textual antecedent. Here are further examples:

(32) At Kyle-na-no under *that ancient roof*
(33) driven out/To climb *that stair* and eat *that bitter bread*
(34) While on *that old grey stone* I sat
(35) Dry timber under *that rich foliage*
(36) Whence did all *that fury* come?
(37) *Those great sea-horses* bare their teeth
(38) Swear by *those horsemen,* by *those women*
(39) Upon the Norman upland or in *that poplar shade*
(40) Swept the sawdust from the floor
 Of *that working-carpenter*

With a textual antecedent, the force of the presupposition in each case would doubtless be weakened by the proximity of a more obvious (textual) source of identification. In these cases, however, the presuppositional dimension is emphasised. For example, in (37) and (38) there is the emphatic presupposition that the reader or allocutor has a shared knowledge which identifies 'Those great seahorses', 'those horsemen', and 'those women'. The identifying facts are felt to belong to a shared body of knowledge, a kind of mythology. Often such noun phrases emphasise a known myth which the poem draws on, as in (38) or (40). But, even with other subject matter – as in (32), (33), (34), (35), (37), and (39) – by emphasising the presupposed status of noun phrases, the anaphoric demonstrative sets up a frame of reference which is *like* a myth in that the identities of the components are not questioned.

In the operation of the mask in these noun phrases, the strength of presupposition as a mode of identification plays against a whole range of forces arising from another mode, namely, the situational. The potential of the demonstrative for situational identification arises from certain intrinsic qualities of that determiner. These qualities set it off from *the*, for example, which though it operates situationally nevertheless does not do so by using *new* knowledge as the demonstrative does. (The difference can perhaps be sensed if *the* is substituted for *that* or *those* in examples (31) through (40) above.)

The situational qualities or powers of the demonstrative can be seen working within the very mechanisms that bring out the presuppositional qualities in its anaphoric use. Consider a hypothetical example, a letter that begins: 'Dear——, That tree is covered with blossoms . . .' 'That tree' obviously refers to something the writer presupposes is known to the receiver of the letter. In fact, the noun phrase might easily be accompanied by reference to the occasion of their common knowledge, as in 'That tree which we saw last summer' or 'That tree which you mentioned in your last letter'. The noun phrase as it stands in the letter could have its identification in either of these ways – a previously experienced situation or a mention in a part of the discourse previous to the letter we have. There is a difference, however, in the two suggested identifying modifications for 'That tree'. 'That tree which we saw last summer' actually identifies the *situation* or *occasion* when the tree became known to the receiver of the letter. In doing so, it seems to provide complete identification for the tree.[8] On the other hand, 'That tree which you mentioned in your last letter' seems to call for still more identifying information. Or, to put it differently, there is the feeling that there has been an additional identifying situation other than the textual one, and this situation is not referred to. The demonstrative has the effect of either suggesting the actual identifying situation or else implying the existence of one. Hence, the second suggested modifier – 'which you mentioned in your last letter' – is felt to be incomplete, or non-defining.[9]

The demonstratives, then, can be said to be somehow 'intrinsically' situational. Their identifying power is tied to a situation, even if it is only an implied one, where or when the identifying knowledge came into being. In situational use, the demonstratives not only require that the attention of the hearer be focussed on the object to be identified; they themselves forge the nexus between the focus of the hearer's attention and the object to be identified. The way they create this nexus is crucial to the operation of the masks, for in many Yeatsian examples the qualities creating this situational nexus come into conflict with the demonstrative's presuppositional aspects.

The demonstratives create situational nexuses with what may be thought of as two separate components. The first is simply an emphatically *directional* quality that may be thought of as the verbal equivalent of pointing. The second component has to do with *distance*. It operates through the opposition of *near/far* and is reflected in the choice between *this* and *that*. Now, when the demonstratives are used non-situationally, when they are used anaphorically, these components are not needed to effect the same kind of identifying nexus as in situational use. As a result, both components seem to come to the foreground. But they emerge only to come into conflict with the opposing presuppositional mode. The results are complex, but can be summed up by saying that the presuppositional mode attempts to bring the identifying knowledge *close* to the present textual moment while the situational mode tends to maintain a *distance* along the axis of its directional pointing. The distance is naturally greater if the demonstrative is *that* or *those*, but even with *this* and *these* there is a conflict of sorts with the presuppositional mode. When the demonstratives are used anaphorically, there is a repeated distancing and contraction, a push and pull, felt because of the demonstrative's own intervening situational powers.

The contracting that takes place within the 'presuppositional' pole of these masks is a separate process from the Deleuzian contractions that take place within the series of differences *between* the two poles. On a different level of analysis, the contractions *participate* in the differential tension that produces the mask, as the anaphoric contraction comes into differential relation with the situational expansion or distancing. The 'presuppositional' contracting is a function of that mode of identification, where there is felt the tendency to assimilate or absorb the identifying knowledge as something presupposed. This tendency becomes especially marked when it contrasts, in a mask-producing conflict, with the situational tendency to *distance* the noun phrase from the identifying knowledge of its source.

The mask-producing conflict just described is actually present in all the examples cited that use the anaphoric demonstrative (31–40). But the conflict is especially strong in these additional examples:

(41) When her soul flies to the predestined dancing place . . .
. . . let her come face to face,
Amid *that first astonishment,* with Grania's shade
(42) Fish, flesh, or fowl, commend all summer long
Whatever is begotten, born, and dies.
Caught in *that sensual music* all neglect
Monuments of unageing intellect.
(43) Marbles of the dancing floor
Break bitter furies of complexity,
Those images that yet
Fresh images beget
That dolphin-torn, that gong-tormented sea.

Here the situational distancing and the anaphoric contracting play against one another so as to affect fairly large segments of the text. First of all, the anaphoric demonstratives pull together various aspects of the text preceding so as to create or imply their own antecedents. (A similar process takes place in the more 'presuppositional' examples (31–40), with the difference that those examples more or less conjure up their own texts or mythologies.) The nouns 'astonishment', 'music', 'images' and 'sea' do not occur in the foregoing portions of the texts. Nevertheless they name aspects which are associated with or entailed by foregoing elements. But they do more than that; they actually redefine or rename an entire, complicated, foregoing entity *as* the particular aspect which they themselves name. Thus, in 'Sailing to Byzantium', not only the song of the birds but all the sensual activity commending the life cycle is characterised as 'sensual music'. Similarly, in (41), the scene of the arrival of the dying lady's soul in heaven is summed up as 'that first astonishment'. And in the famous climax of 'Byzantium', the process is doubled: the 'bitter furies of complexity' are contracted anaphorically first as 'Those images . . .' and then as 'That . . . sea'.[10] The demonstrative's anaphoric power simulates the presupposition that we have already made these large equations, that they are to be understood as given. If *the* were used instead, the noun phrase would simply be taken as part of the scene described, as an attendant factor but not the essence of it.

There is a process of contracting, then, in this distillation and bringing together of many aspects into one 'renaming'. The opposing force, the distancing and pointing power of the demonstratives, also comes into play. On the simplest level, the 'distancing' demonstratives place the 'first astonishment', the 'sensual music', the 'image' and the 'sea' apart from the speaker's location. The distance indicated by the demonstrative is always specifically marked as being between the entity referred to and the subject who is referring. (In these examples, such a distance is certainly appropriate: in (41) someone on earth is describing an experience in heaven, in (42) someone on his way to the afterlife is describing the earthly cycle of change, and in (43) someone in the afterlife is describing the unpurified element he has escaped.)

The distancing accomplished by demonstratives is never stable or fixed, simply because of the opposing anaphoric contractive force. This force seems to permeate the dimension and space created by the distancing aspect. It is perhaps for this reason that the subjectivities produced by these masks are also felt within the dimension of 'distance'. Subjects resulting from a differential tension find a location within the semantic dimensions available in the particular mask, for the differential play takes place within the semantic dimensions of the paradigm as well as the syntactic. In this case, the contested 'distance' seems to provide a location. Subjectivity seems to intensify the semantic distance between the simulated speaking subject and the item referred to by the noun phrase. The following are further examples in Yeats:

(44) The holy tree is growing there;
From joy the holy branches start . . .
There the Loves a circle go . . .
In *those great ignorant leafy ways*

(45) An ancient image made of olive wood . . .
To burn *that stump on the Acropolis*

(46) The swan has leaped into the desolate heaven:
That image can bring wildness, bring a rage

(47) A sudden blow: the great wings beating still . . .
The feathered glory . . .
And how can body, laid in *that white rush*

(48) Told of a harsh reproof, or trivial event
That changed some childish day to tragedy . . .
And thinking of *that fit of grief or rage*

(49) A tree . . .
. . . half all glittering flame and half all green . . .
That staring fury and the blind lush leaf

(50) . . . birds in the trees
– *Those dying generations* – at their song

(51) Are nine-and-fifty swans . . .
I have looked upon *those brilliant creatures*

(52) Even where horrible green parrots call . . .
Unwearied eyes upon *those horrible green birds*.

(53) All by their youth undone,
All, all, by *that inhuman
Bitter glory* wrecked

Here, again, as in (41), (42) and (43), the distancing of the items named is in tension with the anaphoric contracting, which, for example, gathers the various aspects of the swan in (47) as a 'white rush' or the various aspects of the half-burning tree in (49) as a 'staring fury'. But the distancing pole is also felt, particularly in its subjective aspects. Often, there is felt a distinctly *emotional* kind of separation or disjunction between a subject and the entity referred to by the noun phrase. The emotional distance takes on various colorations according to the semantic components of the mask itself. In (51) it seems to be admiration and wonder; in (52), horror and disdain; and in (53), a kind of overwhelmed, bittersweet thrill.

The masks produced by the anaphoric/situational difference are particularly dramatic in all these examples that use the 'distancing' demonstratives *that* and *those*. These determiners create masks out of their affinity for both the 'presuppositional' and the situational modes of identification.

2 The Noun Phrase and the Modifier

Masks are also created in the differential play within certain modifiers of the noun phrase. Once again, the cause of the play of differences is to be seen in competing modes of identification. And again, the play of tensions is localised within the carrier of a particular mode of identification. Because of its differential competition with other modes of identification, the *modifying adjective* will fluctuate in and out of the role of identifier for the noun. Under these circumstances, the adjective will continually differ from itself and become a syntactic mask.

To see how this takes place, we must examine the adjective's own mode of effecting identification as well as additional ways by which the definite determiners accomplish their identifying function.

The definite determiner *the* does not contain actual identifying power within it as the demonstratives do. Instead it always indicates that the needed identification is to be found in another element. The possible locations for that element provide a useful classification of the ways *the* does its job. When the demonstratives operate in roughly analogous ways, as with anaphora, the classification applies to them as well. Essentially, there are three possibilities: the preceding context, the noun itself, and the modifier.[1]

With the first possibility, the determiner effects the identification anaphorically. In the second case, the noun is considered its own defining element. A noun can be 'self-defining' if it has a unique referent, as, for example, with *the moon* or *the truth*. This identification, however, can be seen as just another case of anaphora, one where the defining context includes experience common to almost everyone. (The examples just given could be paraphrased as 'the truth as we generally understand that term to apply' and 'the moon that we all know'.) The generic interpretation of *the* sometimes falls into this category. Generic use is most common with species or types of living things, as in: 'Let *the* cage bird and *the* cage bird mate' or 'shake *the* blossom from *the* bud' or 'tear *the* linnet from *the* leaf'. The sense of an individual item is never far off, though, simply because *the* refers to individuals in its other modes of identification. In Yeats, the play between the universal and the particular can often be sensed:

(1) we'd have *the* new friend meet *the* old
(2) *The* craven man in his seat
(3) We have lit upon *the* gentle, sensitive mind
(4) *The* falcon cannot hear *the* falconer
(5) gardens where *the* peacock strays
(6) How can we know *the* dancer from *the* dance?
(7) Love is like *the* lion's tooth

Many cases which at first reading appear to be generic, such as (4) and (6), also have possible contexts for an anaphoric reading. The falcon and the dancer are not just types; somehow they are also the particular ones in the scenes suggested in their respective poems. Nevertheless, at least a part of our total response is to the generic meaning.

Generic meaning can also be conveyed by the indefinite article, as in 'an aged man is but a paltry thing' or 'a man awaits his end/ Dreading and hoping all'. These meanings are analogous to the generic meaning achieved by the use of the null determiner with plurals. In both cases, the need for further identification is greatly reduced. And the simple present tense reinforces the generic meaning. Thus our interpretation of 'a man awaits', etc. (from Yeats's 'Death') will change because of the changed tense and the more specific 'he' of the next line: 'Many times *he died*.'

The third place for the identifying element is in the modifiers within the noun phrase. Assuming there is no explicit antecedent to create an anaphoric reference, if a noun has a modifier, *the* generally tells us that this modifier defines the noun. In 'the blasted oak', 'the future years', and 'the man who dreamed of faeryland', we know which oak, years, and man are meant, not by any previous mention as with the anaphoric function, but by virtue of the defining modifiers. In Halliday's terminology, this is the forward, or *cataphoric*, reference of the definite determiners. The defining modifier may be adjectival ('the *wintry* blast'), phrasal ('the apple *on the bough*'), or clausal ('the symbol *which/Shadows the inherited glory of the rich*').[2] In this last example, we see something else as well. The noun phrase within the relative clause – 'the inherited glory of the rich' – shows that more than one modifier ('inherited' and 'of the rich') may be used for identification.³ Yeats's text abounds with these complex combinations:

(8) The silver apples of the moon
(9) the lidless eye that loves the sun
(10) the lonely height where all are in God's eye
(11) The uncontrollable mystery on the bestial floor
(12) the old storm-broken trees/That cast their shadows
(13) The holy centaurs of the hills
(14) The freckled man who goes/To a grey place
(15) The dead man that I loved
(16) The most exalted lady loved by a man
(17) the grey rock of Cashel
(18) the haystack- and roof-levelling wind,/Bred on the Atlantic
(19) the loveliest woman born/Out of the mouth of Plenty's horn
(20) the holy city of Byzantium
(21) the gold mosaic of a wall
(22) The half-read wisdom of daemonic images
(23) the barbarous clangour of a gong
(24) the brute blood of the air
(25) the black margin of the wood
(26) the whole/Immense miraculous house/The Bible promised us
(27) The consecrated blade upon my knees
(28) The unpurged images of day
(29) the foul rag-and-bone shop of the heart
(30) The many-headed foam at Salamis

These noun phrases seem to hold two or more identifying elements in a kind of balance. But what if one of the modifiers is sufficient to define the noun? With (8), especially in the light of the next line in 'The Song of Wandering Aengus', it would seem that 'of the moon' identifies the apples and 'silver' provides a description of them. In (25), does the wood have another margin besides the black one? In (17), (20), and (28), again, the *of*-phrases seem enough to identify the nouns. (A possible reading of (20) would take 'holy city' as a unit which is specified by the prepositional phrase.) Finally, in (30), though 'many-headed' figures in the theme of the poem ('The

Statues'), the prepositional phrase carries most of the necessary information for locating and identifying the foam. In most of the other examples the weight of identification similarly tips the balance towards one of the modifiers (interestingly, it is usually the one following the noun). There are others, that actually do require both for full identification – for example, the two involving superlatives, (16) and (19), as well as 'the half-read wisdom of daemonic images'.

Now where one of the modifiers is sufficient for identification, the other is thrust into an ambiguous, fluctuating state where it becomes a mask. Although such a modifier will tend toward description, it will not completely abandon its potentially identifying role. Its power as an indentifier seems to fluctuate as the competing power of the other modifier comes in and out of play. (The other modifier is a mask, too, but not as easily recognised as one.) The 'unneeded' modifiers in the examples quoted above take on peculiarly isolated and unstable roles *vis-à-vis* their noun phrases. They continually move in and out of their linkages to their nouns as necessary identification. As masks, the modifiers force their way out of the natural flow of meaning. A related kind of mask is produced with modifiers in other contexts, particularly in anaphoric noun phrases.

THE MODIFIER AND ANAPHORIC DETERMINERS

Halliday noticed the anomalous effect in Yeats's 'Leda and the Swan' of a potentially defining modifier occurring with anaphoric identification.[4] Consider the following:

(31) the great wings beating still
      Above *the staggering girl*, her thighs caressed
      By the dark webs

The word 'staggering' is not needed as identification but nevertheless tries to exercise its own defining power in the noun phrase. The adjective thus becomes a mask in the same way as one which is placed in competition with another modifier. And this seems to be the case whether the adjective in the anaphoric noun phrase adds modification, as in (31), or only changes the modification of the antecedent.[5] The latter possibility is seen in these lines:

(32) I saw a staring virgin stand . . .
When that *fierce* virgin and her Star

The reason that the modifier can become detached or loosened from its identifying role is that anaphoric noun phrases place the burden of identification and modification on their antecedents. Anaphoric noun phrases are a kind of shorthand. Hence they are usually stripped of modifiers, needing only the determiner to make the link backwards. In an example cited earlier, the noun phrase 'the swordblade' in the second mention no longer needs the modifiers 'All-destroying' and 'still/Carried . . .' to identify it. When a modifier does appear in a fully identified structure, its presence is not grammatically required.

The modifier will also stand out and become a mask when the antecedent is only implicit, as it often is in Yeats. Anaphoric noun phrases rarely repeat what is already assumed, and the potentially identifying facts carried by modifiers *are* usually assumed if the noun phrase is anaphoric. The demonstratives and *the* differ in such cases, however. Without an explicit antecedent, *the* will accept a modifier as identification more readily than *that* will. When there is no clear antecedent, *the* more readily switches, with the addition of a modifier, from an anaphoric interpretation implying an antecedent to a cataphoric interpretation. With *that*, the noun phrase has a strong tendency to retain the anaphoric mode – even without an antecedent and with a modifier.

Though noun phrases with *that* are often modified, the modifiers are rarely felt to be defining. This is especially true of adjectives, as in examples like 'that ancient roof', 'that bitter bread', 'that old grey stone', 'that rich foliage', 'Those great sea-horses', 'That staring fury', etc. The demonstrative forces us to infer other identification for the noun rather than take the adjective as defining. The cataphoric use of *that* is rare because the modifier must somehow indicate an identifying occasion to satisfy the nature of the determiner (as in the earlier hypothetical example: 'That tree which we saw last summer').[6] Consequently, when used with anaphoric demonstratives, a modifier almost invariably becomes a mask.

The subjects produced in these adjectival masks, more or less localised in the adjectives themselves, lend a sense of subjectivity to the meanings of those adjectives. The 'added' modifier often seems to carry a subject's feelings or observations into what is otherwise an objectively defined noun phrase. In the examples with two competing modifiers, (8)–(30), the localised subjectivities emerging from the operations of the mask seem to coincide with intrinsically subjective meanings in each of these: 'lidless', 'lonely', 'uncontrollable', 'holy', 'barbarous', 'whole Immense miraculous', 'consecrated', and 'foul'. But even where the meaning of the adjective is not especially subjective – 'silver', 'old storm-broken', 'freckled', 'dead', 'grey', 'haystack- and roof-levelling', 'black', 'unpurged', 'many-headed' – the resonating operations of the mask seem to make the adjective stand out as the special bearer of a subject's attitudes.

In the cases with anaphoric demonstratives, there is perhaps an even stranger effect. The adjective's meaning is similarly permeated with subjectivities. But, in addition, the subjectivities are localised around the point of view which the determiner creates. So the subjective attitudes conveyed by the demonstrative distance, in any of the various dimensions in which it operates, are felt to be supplemented by the 'added' modifiers. For example:

(33) Are nine-and-fifty swans . . .
I have looked upon those *brilliant* creatures
(34) Even where horrible green parrots call . . .
Unwearied eyes upon those *horrible green* birds
(35) All by their youth undone,
All, all, by that *inhuman*
Bitter glory wrecked

In each case, the adjective not only reinforces the emotional distance but lends an additional subjective quality to it. Or, again, in noun phrases such as 'that ancient roof', 'that bitter bread', 'that rich foliage', etc., where the demonstrative has presuppositional force, the adjective seems to bring subjective proof that the noun phrase indicates something emphatically 'known'. The adjective's subjectivity seems to indicate the *manner* of this knowing on the part of a subject.

The demonstrative indicates various sorts of distance between a subject and the referent of the noun phrase, and thus provides various dimensions within which the subjectivities of the modifier mask can resonate. With anaphoric *the*, on the other hand, the same sorts of dimensions or distances are not found. Therefore generalisations about the role of the modifier are not as useful. Since *the* functions solely by pointing to another element, the subjectivity of modifiers with anaphoric *the*'s can be seen in relation to the contexts that define the noun phrases.

Physical settings in Yeats frequently provide the antecedent for anaphoric references. In 'The Wild Swans at Coole', for example, the swans paddle in 'the cold/Companionable streams' of the estate described. Here the added modifiers show a subjective projection of age and loss in contrast with the situation of the swans. Anaphora to natural things is also typical in Yeats, and in these cases the modifiers tend to bring subjectivity into juxtaposition with outer reality. The sea, in early Yeats, for example, is 'the humming sea', 'the dim sea', or 'the wandering sea'. Cuchulain battles 'the bitter tide' and 'The invulnerable tide' (which in the original version was also 'the bitter tide'). In 'The Circus Animals' Desertion', he battles 'The ungovernable sea'. Subjectivity is lent to each of these adjectives.

The following also occur: 'The wandering foam', 'the ravelled seas', and 'the unpeopled waves'. The earth is 'the wandering earth' or 'the labouring world'. Throughout the poems, modifiers appear subjective in relation to heavenly phenomena:

(36) the passing stars
(37) the brilliant moon
(38) the indifferent stars
(39) the dew-dropping sky
(40) the unlabouring stars
(41) the outrageous stars
(42) the embittered sun
(43) the timid sun
(44) the careless planets
(45) the cold and rook-delighting heaven
(46) the scared moon
(47) the changing moon
(48) the elaborate starlight
(49) the moving heavens
(50) the whirling Zodiac

In cases where anaphoric *the*'s must conjure up the contexts needed for their own reference, the modifier still will come into an unstable conflict with that source of identification. So subjectivity will tend to colour these adjectives as well. In 'His Dream', 'the gaudy stern' abruptly appears in the first line with no antecedent. The nature of the modifier makes it unlikely as a defining one, but we cannot be sure. The result is a mask and a play of subjectivity in that adjective. Similarly, the adjective in the phrase 'the living stream', in 'Easter 1916', is ambiguous. The noun phrase may or may not be anaphoric, depending on whether or not the metaphor established by the words 'a stone/ To trouble . . .' provides a strong enough context for an anaphoric reference. Later in the poem, the description of the stream with the living creatures, the horse and the moor-hens, that are actually in it, tends to fix it as something which is appropriately described – but not completely defined – as 'living'.

Often the defining force of the modifier is somewhat stronger. This is true of 'the *fabulous* darkness' (from 'Two Songs from a Play') and of at least the second modifier in 'the star-lit *golden* bough' (from 'Byzantium'). The defining role of the modifier also seems possible in these noun phrases:

(51) the bitter glass
(52) the generated soul
(53) the mounting swan
(54) the widening gyre

With (54), the adjective can be taken as referring to a particular gyre, the gyre which is widening (in 'The Second Coming') toward the destruction of the previous order. On the other hand, we still feel the pull of an anaphoric reading, even though the noun phrase, occurring as it does in the first line of the poem, has no explicit referent. Yet it can be taken as vaguely conjuring up a referent known through Yeats's system. On this reading, the whole focus is on a single gyre: any opposing gyre is not taken into account. The adjective, then, may well be felt as subjective – lending a subject's feeling (dread?) to the noun phrase. The important point is that in a discourse where anaphora seems always a potential source of identification, the status of defining elements is often ambiguous. It is just this situation which allows the modifiers to become masks with various subjective colorations.

Finally, mythologies (including Yeats's own) can provide the needed 'field' for anaphoric reference. Halliday has pointed out the striking number of such noun phrases in 'Leda and the Swan', where the nouns refer anaphorically to the myth presupposed by the title.[7] Although modified noun phrases with other definite determiners occur in the poem (e.g., 'her helpless breast' and 'those terrified vague fingers'), the ones with *the* predominate:

(55) the great wings
(56) the staggering girl
(57) the dark webs
(58) The feathered glory
(59) the strange heart
(60) The broken wall
(61) the burning roof
(62) the indifferent beak

Masks are produced in all the adjectives because of the competing anaphoric mode of identification. But the qualities that the adjectives assume are not by any means equally subjective in intensity. Nor can their varying subjectivities be attributed to a single subject. The modifiers essentially add two kinds of description. One kind, as in 'great', 'dark', 'feathered', 'strange', and 'indifferent', is static. These adjectives (and we can include 'brute' from line 12, also non-defining, though not because of anaphora) all describe the swan. But they do so (perhaps with the exception of 'indifferent') from the point of view of Leda. The subjectivities surrounding them thus appear to belong not just to a speaker of the poem but to a mind he is dramatising. The effect is as though Leda, helplessly submitting to the bird, reserves a part of her mind for observing it. That part of her mind is what these modifiers give us. (Other features of the poem show a split subjectivity also, for example, the adjectives 'terrified' and 'vague', modifying her fingers.)

The adjectives derived from present participles – 'staggering' and 'burning' – are not static but kinetic. ('Loosening', in a different anaphoric structure, belongs with these.)[8] The descriptions they add set the event in motion but, paradoxically, arrest it at the same time. The inflection *-ing*, which also forms the so-called 'progressive present tense', indicates continuing action. But once the girl is characterised as 'staggering', it is difficult to imagine her any other way. And the same with the other participial adjectives. Other verbal forms also tend to represent motions in an arrested state: the participles in absolute constructions ('beating', 'caressed', 'caught') and the ones in non-restrictive modifiers ('laid', 'caught up', and 'mastered').[9] So the effect of all these forms is to present something like the observed, frozen action on Keats's urn. Any subjectivities felt in the participial adjectives are absorbed semantically by a distanced observer, an almost deliberately impersonal speaking subject. Any remainder of subjectivity in these syntactic masks is probably cancelled by opposing semantic demands, demands which arise from the normal interpretation of the participles. J. Kristeva describes such participles and their lack of subjectivity:

> Les formes nominalisées ou adjectivées du verbe, si elles marquent un proces, ne lui attribuent aucune caractéristique *personnelle* et *temporelle*. Il s'agira donc d'une signifiance qui n'est pas localisée dans un sujet (destinateur) et par conséquent ne s'adresse pas à un locuteur (destinataire) désigné; elle se soustrait à l'ordre de la communication actualisée et se retire dans un hors-sujet, dans une extra-subjectivité où l'action est à l'état 'virtuel' opposé à l' 'actuel' . . . .[10]

So, in this brief poetic text, there are modifiers with vastly differing intensities of subjectivity – and syntactic masks both reinforced and opposed by the normal interpretations of language.

THE MODIFIER AND THE NULL DETERMINER

Besides singular and plural, the English noun has a third category affecting the identification of nouns. This category is the count/noncount status of the noun. Nouns such as 'tranquillity', 'air' and 'imagination' refer to things that are not countable and are therefore called noncount nouns. They appear singular in form (without the *s*-inflection) and are preceded by the null determiner. These nouns are unusual in that in many contexts they do not need any identification. Against this normal pattern, what we find very frequently in Yeats are modifiers added to noncount nouns.

(63) common greenness
(64) supernatural right
(65) most bitter wrong
(66) bitterer sleep
(67) aimless joy
(68) passionate intensity
(69) excited reverie
(70) inanimate phantasy

(71) ancient ceremony
(72) unageing intellect
(73) Excited, passionate, fantastical/Imagination
(74) bursting dawn
(75) dull decrepitude
(76) slippered Contemplation
(77) self-delighting reverie
(78) articulate speech
(79) wholesome sun
(80) blear-eyed wisdom
(81) unknown thought
(82) sibylline frenzy
(83) abstract hatred
(84) storm-scattered intricacy
(85) Primordial Motherhood
(86) numb nightmare

In all such cases, just as with the anaphorically defined nouns, there is a strong source of identification other than the modifier. Here it is the noncount noun itself. So once again the modifier will tend to move in and out of an identifying role in the noun phrase and become a mask.

But what exactly are the reasons for this? Surely a noun like 'sun' or 'dawn' can be modified without any conflict arising. Some noncount nouns, including many of those which refer to masses or substances, do not resist modification as noncounts: for instance, 'cold water' or 'white sand'. These same nouns do, however, in varying degrees resist becoming count nouns. Such expressions as 'a water' or 'a sand' are infrequent. Other noncount nouns, including most of the examples above, readily take on count interpretations. For this reason, expressions like 'a joy', 'an intellect', 'a speech', etc., are not unusual. But these nouns tend to resist modification *as noncounts*. As noncounts their references are more or less general but are fixed and stable. They tend therefore not to allow the particular discriminations made by identifying adjectives (though some can easily occur with *intensifying* adjectives, as in 'sheer joy', 'mere phantasy', or 'utter hatred'). Modifying adjectives with these nouns will tend to become masks.

In normal speech, when identifying shades of meaning must be indicated for noncounts, the needed adjective is usually preceded by one of the determiners (*a* or *the*) which, unlike 'null', indicate that the noun is one which requires identification (*the* showing also that the requirement has been met). Examples of this normal usage are readily found in Yeats.

(87) An aimless joy is a pure joy
(88) An intellectual hatred
(89) a common wrong or right
(90) a humorous happy speech
(91) the pagan speech I made
(92) the endless reverie
(93) The chief imagination of Christendom
(94) the wild thought

Since overt determiners (as opposed to 'null') easily justify the presence of identifying adjectives, the strangeness of examples (63)–(86) naturally disappears if *a* or *the* is prefixed to them. In restricting the generality of the noun's reference, in most cases the use of adjective plus determiner (including *the*, which occurs with both count and noncount nouns) imparts a count interpretation.

In examples (63)–(86), however, the noun phrases do not occur with determiners and do preserve their noncount status. But by doing so they create a conflict within themselves, a conflict between the identifying power of the modifiers and the semantic resistance of the nouns as noncounts to modification. So, once again, there is a conflict between modes of identification producing syntactic masks.

The conflict may tend toward two resolutions, which can be described by noting the scope of 'null' in each case. If 'null' can be taken as governing the noun head alone, then that noun retains its independent meaning and its self-defining quality and the adjective becomes 'detached' from the noun phrase. A similar thing was seen in the modifier's behaviour with anaphorically defined nouns. If the scope of 'null' extends to the entire noun phrase, with the whole noun phrase becoming a null-determined entity, a peculiar compression takes place. In the forcing together of the particularity carried by the modifier and the generality intrinsic to the noun, a new 'word' is created, one which captures a complex meaning. But both resolutions are necessarily partial, given the grammatical forces in opposition. And it is just this instability that allows the masks to be produced.

The same kind of conflict produces masks in other modified noun phrases. Proper names, though obviously not noncount nouns, are almost always self-defining. Nevertheless, in Yeats we find them preceded by adjectives. The adjectives will tend to remain outside the scope of 'null'. But there is a constant vibration toward the kind of compression noted above. The compression usually results in the adjectives taking on the quality of epithets – descriptions which almost become names.

(95) mighty Cuchulain
(96) Wandering Aengus
(97) great Juan
(98) Black Minnaloushe
(99) Greek Alexander
(100) holy Dionysus
(101) Solider Aristotle
(102) World-famous golden-thighed Pythagoras
(103) stately Pythagoras
(104) Tall Pythagoras
(105) buried Hector
(106) great Hector
(107) Great Europa
(108) wild Jack
(109) many-minded Homer
(110) Bland Rhadamanthus
(111) gentler Phidias
(112) half-awakened Adam
(113) bare Ben Bulben

Other modifier-masks are created in Yeats when count nouns are treated essentially as noncounts. Normally, the null determiner does not accompany a singular count noun. However, in Yeats, this convention is frequently broken; that is, singular count nouns often appear without their expected determiners. The effect is that they acquire an interpretation similar to that of noncount nouns. In the lines 'a raving autumn shears/Blossom from the summer's wreath', 'Blossom' gains two interpretations it normally does not have, both of them because it is treated as a noncount noun. We read it as a mass noun – meaning some kind of blossoming substance which is sheared by autumn – but also as an abstract quality, perhaps similar to colour.[11] Frequently the meaning of count nouns does not allow the 'substance' interpretation; but in Yeats we constantly find count nouns which seem to refer to abstractions or qualities. In 'Leda and the Swan', in the line 'And how can body, laid in that white rush', 'body' is stripped of the expected 'her'. The effect is almost to raise the particular body to a generalised state of being, to make the word 'body' mean 'corporeality'. Made into abstractions or qualities, 'body' and 'soul' ('unless/Soul clap its hands') are common in Yeats – as are 'heart' ('though heart might find relief') and 'mind' ('Mind moved yet seemed to stop'). The masks are produced with such nouns when modifiers are added. For example:

(114) ambitious heart
(115) unmeasured mind
(116) falling wave
(117) running crowd
(118) timid brain
(119) heroic mother moon
(120) mountain steep
(121) dripping stone
(122) new moon
(123) flattering tongue
(124) scented lime
(125) painted panel
(126) Quattrocento finger
(127) passing bird
(128) All-destroying sword-blade
(129) great cathedral gong
(130) Common bird or petal
(131) stormy shore
(132) painted stage

The conflict here is not as powerful as it is with the intrinsically noncount nouns, since the count nouns have a naturally greater affinity for modification. But the null determiner nevertheless brings about the same two potential readings as when normal noncounts are forced together with modifiers.

The conflict also takes place with modifiers coming after the noun. Both relative clauses and *of*-phrases are common in Yeats.

(133) peace that comes at length
(134) Beauty that we have won
(135) strength that could unbind
(136) Pleasure that comes with sleep

(137) blossoming or dancing where/The body is not bruised
(138) Brightness that I pull back/From the Zodiac
(139) dark that ran/Down every withered finger
(140) Odour of blood when Christ was slain
(141) changing of night and day
(142) Harshness of their desire
(143) In glory of changeless metal
(144) Perfection of the Life
(145) Supersession of breath
(146) magnanimity of its own desire
(147) extravagance of breath
(148) triumph of intellect
(149) Completeness of their passions
(150) Honey of generation[12]

And, finally, adjectives and postnominal modifiers may both appear–with the conflict affecting both.

(151) Decrepit age that has been tied to me
(152) horrible splendour of desire
(153) ancestral night that can . . . /Deliver from the crime
(154) Symbolical glory of the earth and air
(155) sudden thunder of the mounting swan
(156) Cloudy leafage of the sky
(157) Profane perfection of mankind

With both types of modifier present, the question arises (as we saw with cataphoric noun phrases) as to the priority of one or the other as the chief defining element. At times, a balance between the claims of the two seems to be produced by the compression which results when 'null' is taken as governing the entire noun phrase, that is, when the conflict is given one of its possible resolutions. But the balance is always uneasy and no resolution is ever final.

3 The Relative Clause

There is nothing in the structure of an adjective which marks it as defining or non-defining. An adjective is normally thrust into one role or the other according to whether or not its noun needs it for identification. But the form of the adjective is always the same. With another type of modifier in English, the relative clause, there are distinct formal signals which normally indicate which of the two functions the modifier is filling. Relative clauses exhibit a division of labour, with restrictive clauses helping to define their noun heads and non-restrictves providing a grammatical form especially suited for adding descriptive commentary. In ordinary language these two functions are kept fairly well separated. But there is a usage typical of Yeats's text that complicates their relation and results in syntactic masks.

Both types of clause are usually thought of as sentence-like structures (i.e., clauses) which have been embedded or inserted in other, main, sentences. The relative pronoun provides a necessary link by replacing, in the embedded clause, a noun phrase which is identical to one in the main clause. The relative pronoun thus substitutes for a noun phrase in the embedded clause that would otherwise stand as an unnecessary repetition of a noun phrase in the main clause. The embedded clause, once linked by a relative pronoun, becomes a relative clause. The process can be represented like this:

(1) the man [*the man* made the song] was blind→
 the man *who* made the song was blind

(2) the women [I picked *the women*] spoke sweet and low→
 the women *that* I picked spoke sweet and low

The difference between restrictive and non-restrictive relative clauses appears to depend on whether the embedded clause is linked just to a noun phrase in the main clause or to the main clause itself. A restrictive relative, such as 'who made the song' in (1), is considered a part of the noun phrase it modifies, whereas a non-restrictive would not be considered part of any noun phrase.

If the relationships between sentence parts are represented by a branching structure, the difference can be shown as follows.[1] The italicised parts, terminating branches, are those which would be realised in the actual sentences.

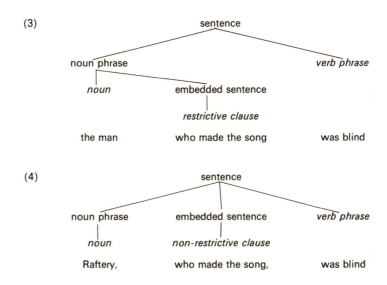

In both cases the relative clause follows directly upon the noun. But the branch representing the relative clause is attached within the noun phrase if the clause is to be restrictive and within the main sentence if the clause is to be non-restrictive.

The diagrams reflect what we know to be generally true of the two types. Restrictives contribute to the identification of their noun phrases while non-restrictives do not; the latter seem to add information relating to an already defined noun to the whole utterance. Both kinds of clause essentially are convenient ways to add the information of one sentence to that of another. But the relative's structure is such that this information can, potentially, be added very specifically to a noun phrase, as in (3), thereby becoming a defining element within it.

Whether or not this option is taken is indicated in the spoken language primarily by the degree of phonetic unity binding the two elements, noun and clause.² A restrictive clause is not separated from its noun head by any marked pause or other sound feature. A non-restrictive *is* set off from the main sentence contour by certain specific phonetic features, including pauses. The writing system indicates these features with commas.

Halliday has shown that the pause separating a non-restrictive clause from its noun head is actually functional in effecting the intended meaning. Halliday observes that such pauses are a specific instance of a more general operation in English. All our speech is segmented by pauses. But the pauses can occur anywhere, and the decision as to where they are placed is significant. By placing a certain stretch of speech between pauses we mark it as a meaningful unit of the total message (the segments most often coinciding with sentences). The making of these 'information units', as Halliday calls the segments, 'represents the speaker's blocking out of the message into quanta of information, or message blocks'.³ For example, the following seems to consist of one information unit (the unit boundaries are marked with the double bar):

(5) //I made my song a coat//

But a sentence may easily have more than one unit:

(6) //I will arise and go now, //and go to Innisfree, // . . .

With relative clauses, the non-restrictive, being set off by pauses, forms a separate information unit; the restrictive is most often included in the same segment as the noun head. The examples given above, in their most likely readings, would break down as follows:

(7) //the man who made the song was blind//
(8) //Raftery//who made the song//was blind//

The inclusion of the relative clause in the same unit as the noun is a *grammatically* functional decision. In (7), the grouping together of an item potentially requiring identification (the noun) with an item which is potentially defining (the clause) is enough to yield the structural fact that the defining relation is present and that the two elements together form a grammatical unit – a noun phrase. In (8) this unit is not formed. So with relative clauses, as Halliday notes, 'information structure determines sentence structure'.⁴

The choice of forming a single unit, of including the clause with the noun in a single noun phrase, is based on the noun's need for the identification the clause can contribute. A noun fully defined by another means will not include a relative clause in its information unit; it will not occur with a restrictive relative clause. The clearest cases are proper nouns and personal pronouns. Since they are almost always easily identified without the help of modifiers, they form independent noun phrases by themselves. Any relative clauses following them will be non-defining, as in (8) – or these:

(9) Fand, who could change to an otter or fawn, . . .
(10) But I, whose virtues are the definitions
     Of the analytic mind, can neither close . . .

For the same reason, a noun defined by anaphora will not need a relative in the defining function. In Yeats's 'The Ballad of Father O'Hart', a noun phrase defined by anaphoric reference to the antecedent 'a shoneen . . .' is quite properly followed by a non-restrictive clause:

(11) the shoneen,/Whom the devils have by the hair

The antecedent happened to include a restrictive relative clause.

(12) a shoneen who had free lands

While this relative clause does not effect a complete identification – which would have been indicated by a definite determiner in the place of 'a' – it nevertheless contributes to the identification of the noun, restricting its possible application.

In a noun phrase with a restrictive clause, the determiner, definite or indefinite, indicates the speaker's judgment about the definiteness of the entire noun phrase (the noun head plus whatever identification the clause contributes). A non-restrictive clause, however, will not influence the definiteness indicated by the choice of determiner, since the non-restrictive is not included in the noun phrase unit. In (11) the clause could have been omitted and 'the shoneen' would still have had a clear and definite identification. By contrast, if a restrictive clause is taken away from a noun with a definite determiner, presumably the noun will no longer be sufficiently or accurately identified. The noun would therefore no longer deserve the definite marking given by the determiner. Consider example (7) in the context from which it was taken, Yeats's 'The Tower', section II. If (7) were stripped of the restrictive clause, becoming 'the man was blind', the noun phrase would not refer as it should to the blind poet who wrote the maddening song mentioned fifteen lines earlier. Instead it would seem to refer, erroneously, to the immediately preceding line of the poem – to the man 'drowned in the great bog of Cloone'. So the restrictive clause has provided needed identification.

Though a non-restrictive does not influence the definiteness of the noun the way a restrictive does, the noun phrase preceding a non-restrictive must possess a certain degree of definiteness on its own. In order for the clause to give the kind of commenting, non-identifying information that non-restrictives are felt to give, the noun must be already identified, at least to some degree. For this reason, the indefinite determiners are unusual in combination with non-restrictive clauses. When, in certain contexts, they do occur with non-restrictives, the clause seems to force some degree of definiteness in the noun phrase. Thus the plural indefinite determiner will often impart a generic interpretation – as in this slightly altered example from Yeats:

(13) To dream of *women*, whose beauty [is] folded in dismay . . . is a burden not to be borne

A singular indefinite determiner co-occurring with a non-restrictive clause yields either the generic interpretation or else a meaning something like 'a certain . . .':

(14) Come out and dig for *a dead man*,/Who's burrowing somewhere in the ground

When it comes to interpreting relative clauses as one type or the other, what precedes the clause – the noun plus the determiner – varies in usefulness as a guiding signal. In a situation where the main formal distinguishing device, the unit-boundary pause, is somehow obscured, a relative clause following a proper noun or a personal pronoun would usually be judged non-restrictive, and one following an indefinite noun would be judged restrictive. The context and the kind of information contained in the clause would help in borderline cases. But with nouns determined by *the* or a demonstrative the decision would be much more difficult.

With potentially anaphoric determiners, the decision about a following relative involves the location of the noun's source of identification. If there is a clear antecedent, as in example (11), then the determiner is clearly anaphoric, the noun is identified in that way, and the clause is non-restrictive. However, antecedents are frequently implicit in Yeats's poetry rather than explicit. In these cases there is the possibility, especially with *the*, that the modifier (the relative clause) rather than an implied antecedent will be accepted as the source of identification. The less clear an implied anaphoric reference is, the more the status of the relative clause must be decided on the basis of formal markers – for example, the comma intonation.

In the following the punctuation is decisive:

(15) the birds, who cry aloud/Their momentary cries before it is dawn
(16) the wood-woman, whose lover was changed to a blue-eyed hawk

In (15), the comma alone shows that 'the birds' is defined by anaphora to those of a particular situation or of common knowledge. In (16), the reference is to a myth. But the only indication that 'the wood-woman' is uniquely identified by anaphora is the comma marking the unit boundary. Without the comma, the determiner would switch to the cataphoric function and the clause would be taken as identifying a particular wood-woman among a possible plurality of wood-women.

In this example –

(17) Would I could cast a sail on the water
Where many a king has gone –

the mode of identification for 'the water' could be *either* anaphoric or cataphoric. The noun's meaning allows anaphoric identification by reference to common experience. Accordingly, the clause can be read non-restrictively. However, if the line ending is not taken as punctuating the unit-boundary pause, the clause becomes restrictive.

The ambiguity caused by positioning the clause at the start of a line is analogous to the ambiguity of the adjectives discussed in the last chapter. And it creates a kind of mask in many of Yeats's relative clauses that is precisely analogous to the masks in those adjectives. In both cases we find a modifier fluctuating between the defining and the non-defining role. Here are more examples:

(18) the starry men,
Who follow with the optic glass/The whirling ways
(19) The Druid, grey, wood-nurtured, quiet-eyed,
Who cast round Fergus dreams
(20) the wayward twilight companies
Who sigh with mingled sorrow and content
(21) the shades of holy men
Who have failed, being weak of will,
Pass the Door of Birth again
(22) that reed-throated whisperer
Who comes at need
(23) What portion in the world can the artist have
Who has awakened from the common dream
(24) Said that wild old wicked man
Who travels where God wills
(25) that raving slut
Who keeps the till

In each of these, the segment preceding the relative clause forms a structure which can stand alone as an independent noun phrase. But it can also accept the following relative clause as a part of the noun phrase, that is, as a restrictive modifier. The arrangement of the lines produces a pause which may or may not be taken as marking a unit boundary after the noun-plus-determiner segment. Hence, the status of the clause – whether or not it is to be included in the same grammatical information unit as the noun – is completely ambiguous. Like the adjective mask, the relative clause encompasses within itself an unresolvable ambiguity, a difference that creates a mask.

The exact operation of the grammatical ambiguity is in fact even more complex. What happens in cases like (17)–(25) is that the prosodic pauses, created by the verse structure, fall in positions where, in the spoken language, pauses have a potential grammatical meaning. Viewed most simply the pause can be either assigned its grammatical meaning or else neglected. That is, the pause can be taken as punctuation (the equivalent of the comma indicating the pause before a non-restrictive) or else it can be considered *not* to have this grammatical function, to have only a rhythmical one. But the actual effect is ambiguous. For the pause inevitably affects the interpretation of the grammatical structure while not actually determining it unambiguously. The result is that a relative clause used in this way takes on aspects of both non-restrictive and restrictive uses without fully becoming one type or the other. But there are also other reasons for this ambiguity.

The clause cannot be interpreted as completely restrictive because of the pause created by the line ending. But what prevents us from hearing this pause as a non-restrictive signal? First of all, the noun-plus-determiner segment, e.g., 'that wild old wicked man', is not unambiguously identified and so does not unambiguously announce that a following relative will be non-restrictive. Then there is the confusion of prosody and speech conventions. Many pauses occurring at the line endings of poetry do not have grammatical meaning, so it is necessary to seek other markers to decide these cases. Punctuation in Yeats often does not follow the conventions we are used to either.[5] Many times in Yeats, as in (18), even the presence of a comma before the clause is not felt to be decisive. So, given the absence of clear signals, we simply do not know if the clause is non-restrictive.

Not knowing if the clause is non-restrictive, we deprive the lines of another intonational feature which is typical of non-restrictive clauses. Consider these clearly non-restrictive examples:

(26) Raftery, who made the song, was blind.
(27) I, who had sat/Dumbfounded before a knave

In these, the segments preceding the clauses – 'Raftery' and 'I' – are given a particular *intonation contour*. Even in rapid pronunciation the voice starts on a high tone, falls, and then rises again, perhaps not quite to the same pitch as initially. This is the typical contour for a noun phrase preceding a non-restrictive. Moreover, the clause itself takes on the same contour.

In any information unit, the component receiving the main stress will usually carry the main intonational characteristics for the entire unit.[6] In (26) and (27), the stressed words 'Raftery' and 'I' coincide with information units. The way these and the other information units are deployed in (26) and (27) can be indicated as follows. Stressed words are italicised.

(28) //*Raftery*// who made the *song* //was *blind*//
(29) //*I*// who had sat Dumbfounded before a *knave* // . . . //

In speaking these lines, the most likely pronunciations for 'song' and 'knave' will echo the high-low-high contours given to 'Raftery' and to 'I'. But 'blind' simply has a falling intonation.

Now, in examples like (17)–(25), this kind of concord between the intonations of two separate units is not present. Or if it is present, it is considerably weakened. As we finish reading the first line of one of these examples, having had no signal that a non-restrictive is to follow, we pause and continue reading the second line with more or less the same level tone. The feeling is that the second line, the relative clause, is a continuation of the first line. The clause has a characteristic of restrictive modification in that it shows a 'unity of intonation contour' with the preceding line, rather than the 'fresh intonation contour' which would characterise a non-restrictive clause.[7]

Thus, because of Yeats's characteristic line arrangement, one formal feature of each type of clause is suppressed while one feature of each type remains in effect. In the following schema, the brackets mark features that are effectively cancelled out by the Yeatsian arrangement:

	Restrictive	*Non-restrictive*
Juncture	[absence of pause]	pause
Pitch	intonation contour shared with noun head	[fresh intonation contour]

The Yeatsian arrangement forces a feature of each type into the same relative clause.

Another way to describe the ambiguity of these clauses is that they alternately fulfil what could be called the 'commenting' and the 'completing' functions normally carried out by non-restrictives and restrictives respectively. In reading, say, example (24), we sense a wholeness as we finish the first line; we feel that 'that wild old wicked man' is a complete noun phrase. However, as we encounter the relative clause on the second line, we are forced to change our perception. What was thought to be complete now seems only partial, and we are forced to accept the clause as additional completing of the noun phrase. But the pause makes the change in our perception difficult, and enforces the commenting nature of the clause. The completing which takes place is thus felt as an uneasy one, one which is somehow forced.

Besides the complex arrangement of intonational signals, another way the relative clause can become a mask is through Yeats's characteristic use of *that* as a relative pronoun.[8] In examples like 'Homer *that* was a blind man' and 'Cuchulain *that* fought night long with the foam', the pronoun, normally used only with restrictives, conflicts with the demands of the proper noun, normally accompanied only by a non-restrictive. The result is that the clause, being read as both restrictive and non-restrictive, becomes a mask. The use of *that* as a relative pronoun also extends to many cases in Yeats where the noun could take either type of clause:

(30) the burnished dove
 That moans and sighs a hundred days
(31) In pools among the rushes
 That scarce could bathe a star
(32) The labyrinth of her days
 That her own strangeness perplexed
(33) Until the axle break
 That keeps the stars in their round
(34) To take my fancy like the wind
 That nobody can buy or bind
(35) Suddenly I saw the cold and rook-delighting heaven
 That seemed as though ice burned
(36) The unavailing outcries and the old bitterness
 That empty the heart
(37) Where, where but here have Pride and Truth,
 That long to give themselves for wage
(38) that stern colour and that delicate line
 That are our secret discipline
(39) I would be ignorant as the dawn
 That has looked down
(40) May God be praised for woman
 That gives up all her mind
(41) That crafty demon and that loud beast
 That plague me day and night
(42) I choose upstanding men
 That climb the streams
(43) Protected from the circle of the moon
 That pitches common things about

(44) The Father and His angelic hierarchy
     That made the magnitude and glory there
(45) I gave what other women gave
     That stepped out of their clothes
(46) Love is all/ Unsatisfied
     That cannot take the whole
(47) Sing the lords and ladies gay
     That were beaten into the clay

As in examples (17)–(25), the line structure in these cases is manipulated so that the line boundary is constantly interacting with the potential unit-boundary pause. The result, again, is that the completing force of the clause (all the stronger with *that* as pronoun) is continually switching in and out of operation.

Many relative clauses in Yeats neither coincide with the line boundary nor employ *that* in a non-standard way. But syntactic masks may also arise with these other clauses. An extremely complex example occurs in the following lines from the last stanza of 'Among School Children'.

(48) Labour is blossoming or dancing where
     The body is not bruised to pleasure soul

As they interact grammatically, the clause and a number of other elements in these lines become masks.

There are several factors complicating these lines. First of all, the *where*-clause, in addition to its role as a relative clause modifying the nouns 'blossoming' and 'dancing', can be taken as an adverbial modifier of the entire main clause. Moreover, 'blossoming' and 'dancing' can be either gerunds or parts of the verb formed with 'is', and the clause, as an adverbial modifier, can go with either the gerund reading or the verb reading. Since adverbial modifiers may be preposed, these two possibilities may be seen more easily if we paraphrase as follows:[9]

(49) [In instances] where the body is not bruised to pleasure soul, labour is [or becomes] blossoming or dancing
(50) [In the place] where the body is not bruised to pleasure soul, labour is [now] blossoming or dancing

The poem is complex enough to provide a context for both these meanings as well as for those given by reading the clause as a relative directly modifying 'blossoming' and 'dancing'. Here our concern is primarily with the latter reading.

The following paraphrases will suggest whether each of the following clauses is restrictive or non-restrictive:

(51) *restrictive*: Labour is [the kind of] blossoming or dancing [in which] the body is not bruised to pleasure soul

(52) *non-restrictive*: Labour is blossoming or dancing, [those phenomena in which we find that] the body is not bruised to pleasure soul

In (48), despite the fact that the relative pronoun is on the same line as 'blossoming' and 'dancing', a factor ostensibly favouring the restrictive reading, the clause is going to be ambiguous. In fact, the position of the pronoun in this case helps to create the ambiguity. If the arrangement were like this,

(53) Labour is blossoming or dancing
Where the body is not bruised to pleasure soul,

the *where*-clause would almost certainly be taken either as a non-restrictive or else as an adverbial modifier – as in (49) and (50), but not preposed. With 'where' moved so far away, a restrictive reading would tend to be ruled out because of the nature of the nouns 'blossoming' and 'dancing'. Since null-determined nouns frequently resist modification, the pause in (53) would not readily be 'bridged' by a requirement of the noun head for identification. The actual line arrangement, however, encourages both restrictive and non-restrictive readings. The proximity of the relative pronoun to the noun heads forces the possibility of a restrictive interpretation.[10] But other factors bring the non-restrictive interpretation into play.

There are two main sets of interactions that need to be traced. First of all, the clause becomes non-restrictive for the nouns 'blossoming' and 'dancing' at the same time as it becomes a restrictive modifier for 'Labour'. Secondly, the clause is both non-restrictive and restrictive in relation to the gerunds.

The reading that establishes the relative clause as a modifier of the two gerunds has a rival whereby the clause modifies 'Labour'. A relative clause will tend to seek a single noun phrase to modify. In one possible reading, 'or' can be felt as conjoining the two gerunds as separate *predicates*, each an alternative attribute of 'Labour' ('Labour is blossoming or else labour is dancing'). In this case, the relative clause does not readily apply to the gerunds since they do not form a single noun phrase.[11] Hence, the clause can be taken as applying to 'Labour'.

If the clause were to apply to 'Labour', the reading would have to be a restrictive one.[12] This reading (related in meaning to (49) above) could be paraphrased as follows:

(54) [that kind of] Labour is blossoming or dancing
      [in which] the body is not bruised to pleasure soul

Paradoxically, the very reading which allows the clause to modify 'Labour' allows it also to fill the role (ambiguously) of non-restrictive modifier of the other two nouns – 'blossoming' and 'dancing'. In other words, under the influence of the factors just described – the factors linking the clause to 'Labour' – the clause's close, restrictive tie to 'blossoming' and 'dancing' is broken. It then becomes free to be felt also as a *non-restrictive* relative following those nouns.

'Or' can also fulfil another role, unifying the gerunds within a single noun phrase. With this reading, 'blossoming' and 'dancing' become equated to one another. 'Or' serves as a 'renaming' device, telling us that 'dancing' is another name for 'blossoming'. (This renaming also serves to unite thematically the stanza's key images, the chestnut-tree and the dancer.) In this case the relative clause remains a restrictive modifier of the gerunds grouped in a single noun phrase: 'blossoming or dancing where . . .'.

Within this noun phrase, the clause interacts differently with the two gerunds. While it seems to go smoothly with 'dancing', a conflict is felt if we try to apply it to 'blossoming'. The natural resistance of noncount nouns to restrictive modification is apparently stronger in the case of 'blossoming'. Those noncounts that more readily acquire meaning as count nouns are felt to resist modification as noncounts. And this resistance is true of 'blossoming', which, in fact, becomes count more readily than 'dancing'.[13]

The conflict felt with 'blossoming' may also have to do with the distance between it and the clause. Also the very fact that 'blossoming' comes first may make it seem more alien to modification than 'dancing' is: by the time we read 'dancing', having anticipated its modification longer, the potential conflict between modifier and null determiner is less striking. Perhaps, too, semantic factors increase the conflict in the case of 'blossoming', for, unlike 'dancing', it combines somewhat strangely with a modifier describing human activity. At any rate, the effect of the conflict is that the clause is again given a non-restrictive reading along with its restrictive ones.

The relative clause has a complex ambiguity which springs from its polyvalence in relation to the nouns in the line. The clause interacts differently with each noun, building up and releasing tension as an anticipated restrictive or non-restrictive modification is assigned to and then disengaged from 'Labour', 'blossoming', and 'dancing'. Reading also takes place backward along the line, with the modification of 'Labour' arching backward from the end of the line to the beginning. This modification has an important (perhaps preliminary) impetus when we encounter the word 'or'. In one of its interpretations 'or' forces the clause to modify 'Labour'. But, simultaneously, the noun phrase 'blossoming or dancing' is constituted as a temporary unity, so the tension of 'blossoming' and the ease of 'dancing' are both brought out in relation to the clause.

The upshot of all these interactions is a remarkable network of differential series within the 'single' relative clause. There are several restrictive interpretations differentiating themselves from each other as well as from several non-restrictive interpretations . . . which in turn are continually differentiating themselves from each other and from the restrictives. If we consider all the other elements of the sentence which are differing from themselves in series with all these differences, we begin to have an idea – even in this small stretch of language – of the way differential series can proliferate.

4 Additive Structuring

The masks that come about through 'additive structuring' are basically analogous to those produced in the relative clause. In the relative clause the chief condition was the ambiguous relationship between the clause and its surrounding context. A relative clause that has been made ambiguous will always manage to be a separate unit of information, like a non-restrictive, yet will also succeed in being the completion of what has gone before, like a restrictive. Such clauses are felt to escape from or violate the very structures that initially define them, i.e., the normal interpretations of language. The markers that would point to one type of clause or the other are eliminated, reduced, or placed in an irresolvable conflict. As a consequence, the *raison d'être* of the clause becomes less a meeting of the demands of language and more a function of the differential series that the clause is caught up in.

The most general way to describe the peculiar ambiguity of these clauses would be in terms of the normal demand in English for clear-cut relationships between the segments of the sentence. With the relative clause this demand is consecrated in the hard and fast distinction between the restrictive and the non-restrictive clause. What the relative clause masks succeed in doing is to slip between the poles of this distinction and in general to slip between the demands that a segment be either *tied to* or *separate from* its neighbouring segments. The 'in between' status of these masks is felt in the fact that the clause both completes the preceding noun phrase and takes on an independent role. The clause is oriented to a preceding element but is totally independent of it, possessing an equal strength in the linear progression of units. In such a situation, the clause becomes alien to the normal structure of the language. The clause no longer has either a normal grammatical linkage to or a normal grammatical separation from its context. Left hanging in an agrammatical or *anti*-grammatical space, the clause becomes a syntactic mask.

This way of concatenating the segments of language is pervasive in Yeats, even beyond its use with the relative clause. In a number of different ways, certain kinds of element become alien – like the relative clause – to the normal hierarchical structuring of language, with all its relationships of linkage, domination or subordination. The postnominal modifiers in the following examples (on the second line of each) are close to the relative clauses in the way they relate to their preceding nouns:[1]

(1) I thought of your beauty, and this arrow,
    Made out of a wild thought, is in my marrow
(2) I made my song a coat
    Covered with embroideries
(3) Like some last courtier at a gypsy camping-place
    Babbling of fallen majesty
(4) Over some silken dress
    Cut in the Turkish fashion
(5) There is a waterfall
    Upon Ben Bulben side
(6) For arrogance and hatred are the wares
    Peddled in the thoroughfares
(7) O may she live like some green laurel
    Rooted in one dear perpetual place
(8) To young upstanding men
    Climbing the mountain-side
(9) Even the grey-leaved olive-tree
    Miracle-bred out of the living stone
(10) Sato's ancient blade ...
     Still razor-keen, still like a looking-glass
     Unspotted by the centuries
(11) the tower
     Emblematical of the night
(12) her feet/Practice a tinker shuffle
     Picked up on a street

Here the line endings make two segments, two information units, where there might be only one. But the key condition is that the two segments have a potential but not a necessary grammatical unity.[2] Modifiers such as these are frequently but not always included in the same noun phrase and information unit as their noun heads. Given their ambiguous affiliation, the separation of the two elements leaves their grammatical tie undecidable. Just as with the relative clause, the line break falls at the precise place which will obscure the tie (again, one of various degrees of restriction). So the modifier can do nothing but differ from each of its possible roles in relation to the noun phrase.

At one level of interpretation, these forms appear to escape any other arranging principle except the plain sequence given to them by their physical places in the poem. The spacing caused by the line structure brings out their linear rather than their grammatical concatenation. They form a syntactic chain but one which is disarticulated rather than one structured according to fixed grammatical relationships. This kind of arrangement can be called 'additive structuring'. In reading the modifiers, it is clear that one thing comes after another, but there are no signals as to the grammatical reasons for the sequence. In this kind of structuring, any element may potentially become a mask, since it may be forced into the same sort of ambiguous, anti-grammatical relation to its context that was true of the relative clause.

The arrangement of lines in a poem can thrust additive structuring onto other kinds of syntactic component besides the relative clause or the postnominal modifier. It can also create additive structuring in a different way from that which affects these two kinds of component. For example:

(13) This great purple butterfly,
      In the prison of my hands,
      Has a learning in his eye
      Not a poor fool understands.

(14) I mock Plotinus' thought
      And cry in Plato's teeth,
      Death and life were not
      Till man made up the whole,
      Made lock, stock and barrel
      Out of his bitter soul

(15) Everything that man esteems
      Endures a moment or a day.
      Love's pleasure drives his love away,
      The painter's brush consumes his dreams;
      The herald's cry, the soldier's tread
      Exhaust his glory and his might:
      Whatever flames upon the night
      Man's own resinous heart has fed.

The second line of (13) is a modifying structure like those in (1) – (12) and is thus felt to be additive. But the next two lines also have this effect. In all three examples, in fact, each line tends to be felt as a block in a sequence of *similar* blocks where none has grammatical dominance over another. This has to do with the line structure itself.

While accomplishing a prosodic pattern, the organisation of a poem into lines also establishes a succession of information units. A unit can take on an independence which runs counter to whatever syntactic ties may exist. In the examples above, each line partly becomes a separate and equal block with no necessary connection with the preceding or following blocks. With lines structured as information blocks, each block enters into the mask-producing play, the play between belonging and not belonging to a syntactic role, between fulfilling and not fulfilling the expected tie or absence of tie between elements.

Additive structuring that depends on the line unit seems to take place mainly when the units are relatively short. For this reason, it is particularly noticeable in poems that have short, three- or four-beat lines. When units are longer they approach a certain norm for English – perhaps since the most usual relationship between information units and sentence structure is for a unit to coincide with an entire clause. As Halliday puts it: 'in the unmarked option one information unit is one clause'.[3] Clauses can be quite short, but they are probably longer on the average than most other syntactic constituents. When information units are long they approach the length of unit most natural for speech. At that point, the units are subjected to the demands of syntax and are no longer particularly noticeable as separate units. In the following, for example, the information units more or less correspond to what we would find in spoken language:

(16)   //You are more beautiful than any one,//
       //And yet your body had a flaw://
       //Your small hands were not beautiful,//

The segmentation of these lines is scarcely noticed because it corresponds to a fairly natural speech rhythm. Moreover, the lines have the information unit and the clause coinciding. However, when the information structure of (16) is altered, this is one possible effect:

(17)   //You are more beautiful//
       //than any one,//
       //And yet your body//
       //had a flaw://
       //Your small hands//
       //were not beautiful,//

These lines have a broken, rather breathless rhythm, almost as if formed by a subjectivity continually thinking of new things to say. The information units, being shorter than expected, have an additive quality not present in (16), at least not with the same intensity.

A number of factors can reinforce the unit-boundary pause and help to mark the line as an information unit. The end rimes help, and also the rhythmic regularity of the lines. In both (13) and (14), each line has three stresses, while in (15) each has four. With this regularity, the number of syllables per line is fairly even, too: in (13) each line has seven; in (14) all except one have six; and in (15) they all have eight except one.

Any similarity affecting the line as a whole will have an equalising effect and help define the line as a separate information unit. When the lines coincide with major syntactic constituents, they naturally become marked off as units – even though the constituents may be of different sorts. In (13), for instance, the following occur:

1. a noun phrase
2. a prepositional phrase (containing another prepositional phrase)
3. a verb phrase (with a direct object followed by a prepositional phrase)
4. a relative clause

Example (14) has these components:

1. a main clause (a subject-verb-object sequence that could be taken as complete)
2. a verb phrase (conjoined to the verb phrase of the preceding line)
3. a main clause
4. a subordinate clause
5. a verb phrase
6. a prepositional phrase

And (15) has these:

1. a noun phrase (including a relative clause)
2. a verb phrase
3. a main clause
4. a main clause
5. two noun phrases
6. a verb phrase
7. a noun phrase
8. a noun phrase plus a verb[4]

With the syntax arranged in this way, the various components tend to have equal importance. Each component, whether it be a main clause or a modifier, is given more or less the same emphasis as a sequential block.

Additive structuring may sometimes be sustained for an entire poem. In 'News for the Delphic Oracle', for example, almost every line has a separate syntactic unit.[5] There is set up a strong pattern of similarity based on the coincidence of line and unit. The rhythm, alternating four beats with three, reinforces the pattern. In effect, the expectation and fulfillment of the meter as each unit is read superimposes another kind of ambiguous independence on each unit in the succession of segments. Each unit is both the continuation of the pattern and a self-sufficient block of rhythm. The one line which markedly breaks the syntactic regularity comes almost at the end of the poem. Note the way this line interrupts the pattern:

(18) Down the mountain walls   *prepositional phrase*
      From where Pan's cavern is   *prepositional phrase*
      Intolerable music falls.   *clause*
      Foul goat-head, brutal arm
         appear,   *clause*
      Belly, shoulder, bum,   *noun phrases*
      Flash fishlike; nymphs and
         satyrs
      Copulate in the foam.   *verb phrase*

The line is made up of the verb phrase of one clause followed by the subject noun phrase of another, the last one of the poem. The semicolon separates the last two members in a series of three clauses, and, as a strong syntactic divider, it breaks up the succession of whole units. But possibly another kind of additive structuring takes over at this point in the poem. The interruption of the measured succession of units actually begins two lines before the anomalous line. A more rapid adding of element after element begins here – particularly with the noun phrases 'Foul goat-head', 'brutal arm', and the series 'Belly, shoulder, bum'. Acceleration in the occurrence of information units is itself a form of additive structuring.

Similarity based on the coincidence of line and syntactic unit is both a cause and an effect of additive structuring. For where it is absent or only partial, an additive structuring will often bring it out, even against the resistance of contrary syntactic ties. For most of the lines in 'News for the Delphic Oracle', the play between syntactic independence and affiliation is a smooth and subtle operation. Elsewhere in Yeats the additive structuring often takes place against stronger syntactic ties reaching across line boundaries. Certain lines in the final section of 'The Fisherman' are examples. Up to the fourth line from the end, almost all the lines of the section coincide with syntactic units. Aside from those final four lines, the only questionable ones are the first two lines of the section. These two seem to lack the degree of syntactic completeness that would enable them to participate in additive structuring.

(19)   Maybe a twelvemonth since
       Suddenly I began,

The lines seem tied by virtue of the word 'since'. And the second line ends with a verb that demands a complement. But other readings of the lines fight against these ties and help the segments achieve the ambiguous play necessary to additive structuring. As we come upon the verb 'began', it is possible to interpret it as having a complement occurring *earlier* in the text rather than later—in which case the line seems a completed unit as it stands. The actual complement ('Imagining a man') comes two lines later (after a prepositional phrase).[6] But that affiliation does not completely cancel out the reading just suggested. Rather, the two compete – and help create a mask in the segment ending with 'began'.

An ambiguity also arises in the first line. Along with the reading of 'since' as a subordinating conjunction linking to 'Suddenly I began', another reading would make the line an independent adverbial structure. As an adverbial structure, it could be paraphrased 'Maybe a year after that' or 'Maybe a year since then'. This ('correct') reading refers 'since' back to the first section of the poem, back to the day when the speaker confronted both 'the reality' of writing for his own race and what he had 'hoped 'twould be'. The first line of (19), then, is also an independent constituent, an adverbial phrase. But both this line and the one following it must struggle to be read as independent constituents. They must resist readings which would tie them to neighbouring lines.[7]

From the complement of 'began', all the lines are separate constituents – up to the point mentioned above, the fourth line from the end:

(20) Imagining a man,   *participial phrase*
      And his sun-freckled face,   *noun phrase, conjoined*
      And grey Connemara cloth,   *noun phrase, conjoined*
      Climbing up to a place   *participial phrase*
      Where stone is dark under
          froth,   *relative clause*
      And the down-turn of his
          wrist   *noun phrase, conjoined*
      When the flies drop in the
          stream;   *relative clause*
      A man who does not exist,   *noun phrase*
      A man who is but a dream;   *noun phrase*
      And cried, 'Before I am old
      I shall have written him one
      Poem maybe as cold
      And passionate as the dawn'.

The four final lines obviously break the succession of segments that coincide with syntactic units. The first does this most dramatically: after the verb 'cried' (conjoined with 'began', eleven lines back), a completely new clause begins within the line. The next line begins the main clause of the quoted sentence and ends with the first element (the numeral 'one') of the direct object. The following line has the noun head of the object and the first part of a comparative construction ('maybe as cold') which is completed by the final line of the poem. But except for the line beginning the quoted sentence, all these lines have readings as complete components, too. The readings are forced, but nevertheless part of the ambiguous operation of the lines. The numeral 'one' could be taken as an anaphoric substitute for an antecedent; it thus would be felt as completing its clause as a complete direct object. The next line could be read as a complete noun phrase if the comparative 'as cold' were felt to compare the 'Poem' to something previously mentioned as being cold.[8] And, finally, the last line could be read as a complete modifier (like 'swift as the wind'). With the additive structuring of lines, it would seem that almost any segment can partially loosen its syntactic ties and become a mask, as these components do.

In these examples, *linked* components fluctuate toward the opposite pole, toward independence. It is possible to find the reverse taking place? Units in an additive sequence would be expected to be given the leeway to differ both from dependence and from completeness. Therefore, the mask-producing operation must work in both senses. It must not only increase the self-sufficiency of dependent components (as in 'The Fisherman'), but it must also reduce the self-sufficiency of independent components. In the latter case, the movement among units towards similarity based on wholeness should be undercut. This undercutting is exactly what would be expected of a differential series, where each item must ultimately undercut its sameness from the others and differ. Ultimately, the similarity based on wholeness must be undercut in additively structured discourses, as units become undecidable as to their syntactic affiliation. Any given unit will lose and gain wholeness continually.

The best test-case for observing a unit losing wholeness would probably be a main clause. A main clause would be least susceptible to losing self-sufficiency since main clauses are the most complete syntactic unit. The wholeness of a main clause is more strongly felt than the wholeness of other parts of the sentence. However, even main clauses will become ambiguously related to their contexts if they are detached by additive structuring from the normal flow of discourse. This sort of detaching takes place in the following example. The example has two main clauses, each of which is preceded by two non-clausal segments.

(21) Earth in beauty dressed   *noun phrase*
      Awaits returning spring.   *verb phrase*
      All true love must die,   *clause*
      Alter at the best   *verb phrase* (auxiliary 'must')

      Into some lesser thing.   *prepositional phrase*
      Prove that I lie.   *clause*

Additive Structuring

Here the clauses seem to lose some of their completeness. The completeness would have been felt as a kind of conviction, were it not for the additive sequence. The two clauses – 'All true love must die' and 'Prove that I lie' – ostensibly have great strength; the first is a categorical statement, the second an imperative. But, in an environment of segments lacking the wholeness of main clauses, the clauses take on a tentative quality. The clauses seem to have become susceptible to the influence of the other units in the sequence. The less complete units – though they have a *degree* of completeness in themselves, as noun phrase, verb phrase, etc. – lend a certain incompleteness to the main clauses. The main clauses then fluctuate toward a polar position different from their primary interpretation of completeness. This movement is only possible because the sequence induces in them a state of permeability.

Where normal interpretation wants to see either unambiguous linkages or unambiguous separations, additive structuring gives us both. The units are no longer definable within the stable framework of paradigms consisting of different possibilities. Instead the unit internalises the paradigm by playing out all its possibilities. Like all the masks these syntactic units possess a kind of energy. With units affected by additive structuring, the energy also seems to be passed along the entire chain. A chain of such units becomes permeable through the undecidability of its members. From one point of view, the members of the chain are equalised, levelled, or disarticulated *vis-à-vis* one another. But, from another point of view, they are put into differential relation with one another. An ambiguity in one member will set off the differential play of other members.

Similar chains, with similar effects, are created in Yeats's text by another form of additive structuring. This form also consists of long chains of syntactic units of various kinds. As before, the disarticulation is a direct result of the way units are strung together. But in this case, units are strung together essentially as *conjoined structures*, rather than as separated line units. Since these structures are created primarily by means of conjunctions, this type of additive structuring could be referred to as 'polysyndeton'. The following examples, with the conjunctions italicised, are typical:

(22)   *And* in the trembling blue-green of the sky
       A moon, worn *as if* it had been a shell
       Washed by time's waters *as* they rose *and* fell
       About the stars *and* broke in days *and* years

(23) Had I the heaven's embroidered cloths,
      Enwrought with golden *and* silver light,
      The blue *and* the dim *and* the dark cloths
      Of night *and* light *and* the half-light
(24) I will talk no more of books *or* the long war
      But walk by the dry thorn *until* I have found
      Some beggar sheltering from the wind, *and* there
      Manage the talk *until* her name come round.
      If there be rags enough he will know her name
      And be well pleased remembering it, *for* in the old days,
      Though she had young men's praise *and* old men's blame,
      Among the poor *both* old *and* young gave her praise.
(25) *And* that alone; *yet* I, being driven half insane
      Because of some green wing, gathered old mummy wheat
      In the mad abstract dark *and* ground it . . .
      And after baked it slowly in an oven; *but* now
      I bring full-flavoured wine out of a barrel found
      Where seven Ephesian topers slept *and* never knew
(26) Things said *or* done long years ago,
      Or things I did not do *or* say
      But thought that I might say *or* do,
      Weigh me down, *and* not a day
      But something is recalled,
      My conscience *or* my vanity appalled.

The conjunctions here are analogous to the line divisions of earlier examples in the way they mark syntactic segments. With the repeated use of the conjunction mechanism, the language becomes divided into units which can separate and fall together with a lessened dependence on syntactic hierarchy. Conjoined structures are made from syntactic items which are not parallel and the elements of these structures undergo an equalisation. They gain and lose both affiliation and independence in turn, and they become masks.

There is also the possibility of the line boundaries playing their usual role and reinforcing the work of the conjunctions – especially when the conjunctions come at the beginnings of lines:

(27) *And* no more turn aside *and* brood
      Upon love's bitter mystery;
      For Fergus rules the brazen cars,

Additive Structuring

> *And* rules the shadows of the wood,
> *And* the white breast of the dim sea
> *And* all dishevelled wandering stars.

(28) I went out to the hazel wood,
Because a fire was in my head,
And cut *and* peeled a hazel wand,
And hooked a berry to a thread;
And when white moths were on the wing,
And moth-like stars were flickering out,
I dropped the berry in a stream
And caught a little silver trout.

(29) *And* many a king's daughter,
And alight at the comely trees *and* the lawn,
The playing upon pipes *and* the dancing,
And learn that the best thing is
To change my loves *while* dancing
And pay but a kiss for a kiss.

But the reinforcing will only take place when the lines are relatively short. And this reveals an important difference between polysyndeton and the line-unit mode of additive structuring. Polysyndeton has the capacity to impart additive structuring to long lines as well as short. The information units of ordinary language tend to be longer, on the average, than the length of three- or four-stress lines of poetry. So lines of three or four stresses will often gain an emphasis *as units*. This emphasis allows them their additive role. But since longer lines do not stand out as units, they require other factors if they are to be felt as belonging to additive sequences. Conjunctions can serve this purpose:

(30) *And* we are hurt *if* either friend seem cold,
And there is salt to lengthen out the smart . . .
And quarrels are blown up upon that head;
But not a friend that I would bring
This night can set us quarrelling,
For all that come into my mind are dead.

(31) *And* look most like me, being indeed my double,
And prove of all imaginable things
The most unlike, being my anti-self,
And, standing by these characters, disclose
All that I seek; *and* whisper it

(32) *And* thinking of that fit of grief *or* rage
I look upon one child *or* t'other there
And wonder if she stood so at that age –
For even daughters of the swan . . .
And had that colour upon cheek *or* hair,
And thereupon my heart is driven wild

A final mode of additive structuring institutes the necessary disarticulation simply by interrupting the flow of discourse. There is probably no form of additive structuring as characteristic of Yeats as this one. In this mode, the normal syntactic ties must 'reach over' parenthetical interruptions of various sorts. The interrupting elements play a part that is analogous to line boundaries. The essential difference is that here the interruption arises from an actual stretch of language ostensibly incorporated in the sentence. But the effect is the same. The interruption allows the syntactic ties between the elements on either side of it to be loosened but not broken. The elements themselves then fall into a hovering between affiliation and separation – the endless fluctuation and differing from themselves that makes them masks.

The structures most commonly used as 'interrupters' in Yeats are non-restrictive modifiers. In (31), there are three of them: 'being indeed my double', 'being my anti-self', and 'standing by these characters'. In each case, the sentence structure is interrupted and the elements on either side of the interruption are thrust into the paradoxical status of being both linked and separated from their usual syntactic partners. Another example can be seen in (25), where the interruption ('being driven half insane', etc.) makes both 'I' and 'gathered . . .' into syntactic masks. In the examples that follow the first word of the interrupting structure has been italicised:

(33) But I, *being* poor, have only my dreams
(34) I had thought, *seeing* how bitter is that wind
That shakes the shutter, to have brought to mind
(35) Till, *clambering* at the cradle-side,
He dreams himself
(36) We . . . *being* but the world were best away
(37) And how can body, *laid* in that white rush,
But feel the strange heart
(38) That flowering, silken, old embroidery, *torn*
From some court-lady's dress and round

>   The wooden scabbard bound and wound,
>   Can, *tattered*, still protect, *faded* adorn.
> (39)   Can *like* the cocks of Hades crow,
>   Or, *by* the moon embittered, scorn aloud
> (40)   Nor knew, *drunken* with singing as with wine,
>   That they had brought
> (41)   She, *pity*-crazed, had given her soul away
> (42)   Maybe at last, *being* but a broken man,
>   I must be satisfied with my heart

At times, there are multiple interruptions, and even interruptions within other interruptions. Many kinds of construction – phrases, clauses, appositives, absolutes – can be found along with the non-restrictives in this function.

> (43)   We who still labour by the cromlech on the shore,
>   *The* grey cairn on the hill, *when* day sinks drowned in dew,
>   *Being* weary of the world's empires, bow down
> (44)   I became a man, *a* hater of the wind,
>   *Knowing* one, *out* of all things, alone, that his head
>   May not lie on the breast
> (45)   And all their eyes still fixed, *hoping* to find once more,
>   *Being* by Calvary's turbulence unsatisfied,
>   The uncontrollable mystery on the bestial floor
> (46)   All's changed since I, *hearing* at twilight,
>   *The* first time on this shore,
>   The bell-beat of their wings above my head,
>   Trod with a lighter tread.
> (47)   When, *the* ears being deafened, *the* sight of the eyes blind
>   With lightning, you went from me
> (48)   But that, *long* travelling, he had come
>   *Towards* nightfall upon certain set apart
> (49)   And made – *being* poor, ailing and ignorant,
>   *Shut* out from all the luxury of the world,
>   *The* coarse-bred son of a livery-stable keeper –
>   Luxuriant song.
> (50)   And certain men, *being* maddened by those rhymes,
>   *Or* else by toasting her a score of times,
>   Rose from the table

The device is constant in Yeats and it would be hard to find a poem of his that does not exhibit it in one form or another. As a final example, the poem 'While I, from that reed-throated whisperer' has a single sentence interrupted by several kinds of structure. The sentence begins with a subordinate clause:

(51) While I . . . surmise companions/Beyond the fling of the dull ass's hoof . . . and find . . . A sterner conscience and a friendlier home,

Then comes the main clause (including an appositive which expands the direct object of 'forgive'):

(52) I can forgive even that wrong of wrongs,/Those undreamt accidents that have made me . . . Notorious . . .

The longest interruption is also the first: the prepositional phrase 'from that reed-throated whisperer . . .' which modifies 'surmise'. This interruption is lengthened by a relative clause modifying 'whisperer': 'Who comes at need . . .'.[9] And the relative, in turn, is lengthened by a long adverbial phrase modifying 'comes':

(53) although not now as once/A clear articulation in the air,/But inwardly

The last two words, 'But inwardly', may also be read as belonging primarily to the main part of the relative clause. (This reading would take 'inwardly' as contrasting to 'at need': 'Who comes at need. . . . But inwardly'.) In this case, the adverbial, (53), not only considerably lengthens the distance in the subordinate clause, (51), between 'I' and 'surmise', but it also interrupts the relative clause. (The adverbial itself is interrupted in a minor way by the short adverbial phrase 'as once'.)

There are two other interruptions of (51): first, a parenthetical comment on the phrase about the 'dull ass's hoof',

(54) – Ben Jonson's phrase –

and then an adverbial clause modifying 'find':

(55) when June is come . . .

The main clause, (52), has a two-line interruption within its appositive. The interrupting structure consists of a subordinate clause with a non-restrictive modifier of its subject, 'Fame'.[10]

(56)   —Seeing that Fame has perished this long while,
        Being but a part of ancient ceremony—

The poem ends with a subordinate clause ('till all my priceless things . . .') which must reach back past (56) to the verb phrase 'made me . . . Notorious' in order to find the action it modifies.

From beginning to end, the poem's single sentence is sharply interrupted in four main places. The interruptions take various forms and affect practically every element of the sentence. Major elements which belong together are separated—subject and predicate ('I'/'surmise'), parts of a verb phrase ('surmise'/'and find'), verb and object ('find'/'A sterner conscience'), and parts of a verb phrase complement ('made me'/'Notorious'). But the mask-producing separations can hardly be confined just to these elements. The entire poem seems to undergo disarticulation—the interrupting elements as well as the main sentence parts. Additive structuring by interruption, like the other modes discussed, breaks up a text into segments that lose their univocal grammatical ties.

5 The Grammar of Time in the Mask

What sort of time dimension contains or explains the peculiar occurrence of the syntactic masks? Where does the repetition of these mask-events fit into the usual sense of time and duration? What can be expected of this dimension is that time itself will become something differential since the differential event of the mask cannot take place in other than a differential manner.[1] The mask in its differentiality perhaps even overthrows the notion of 'taking place' in time – unless the mask can be seen as creating its own series of moments in each repetition. But how might it accomplish this? Perhaps the mask can be seen in differential relation to another series of differences which would be 'its' time dimension – an infinite series of divided, differential moments occurring at each repetition of the mask. The mask, if it is thought of as a series of differences, cannot also be placed against a homogeneous 'background' of time or within a homogeneous 'medium' of time. Its differential movement cannot be linked to the kind of time which attempts to encompass both poles of its difference in any single expanded 'present'. Its differential movement does not fit with a continuity of full moments. If there is any present, or 'now', involved in the mask, it can only be a series of minuscule presents spun out of the differential movement itself.

Such a series would not encompass the movement of the mask in any kind of progress or flow. Masks can be spoken of as occurring, being created, taking place, happening, becoming, being produced, etc. – as if their time *were* part of a gradual progression or flow. They can be described as later effects of earlier causes, with both cause and effect belonging to a succession of moments given full, 'present' realities – at different 'positions' in the same flow of moments. Such formulations are based on the platonic vocabulary of pre-existing forms and later contents. But the syntactic masks are not in that kind of relation to the paradigms of language. The mask neither comes after a pre-existing paradigm which 'produces' it, nor does it precede the paradigm and set up the latter as a reflection of its differential structure. The syntactic mask and the paradigm are involved in one another and neither pre-exists its relation to the other. The occurrence of the mask cannot be thought of as an event in a sequence. It must be given another kind of time dimension suitable to its differential operation. One way of conceiving of such a dimension is as another of the series that operate differentially in the mask.

There is one particular type of syntactic mask that makes such a series conceivable and in fact involves such a series as a factor in its operation. The masks that work in relation to time series are the masks of *verbal tense*. Tense is the place in the language where time indications internal to the language are supposed to link up with exterior or 'real' time. The paradigms of tense are articulated normally in terms of this 'real', sequential time. When the paradigms of tense become masks, however, as they very commonly do in Yeats, their time indications are precisely what become differential. The time indication of a given verb will become undecidable in the same way that indications of grammatical affiliation became undecidable in some of the earlier examples. The masks of tense, therefore, dramatise the sort of time that masks create for themselves.

. There is an important functional division among verb tense forms. The English verb tenses have been analysed as having two main functions, the narrative and the non-narrative.[2] With the narrative use, the tenses are employed for the particular purpose of indicating the sequence of definite occasions when events occur in relation to one another and in relation to the moment of discourse at which the tense is used. For example:

(1)   When night *had deepened*,
      I *groped* my way from beech to hazel wood

The past tense in 'groped' indicates that the action took place before the moment of use in the discourse. The past perfect tense in 'had deepened' indicates that the 'deepening' action took place before the time of the action indicated by the past tense.

The narrative use operates in a similar way for sequences in the future and the present:

(2) Before I am [i.e., *shall be*] old/I *shall have written* him one/
Poem
(3) Midnight *has come*, and the great Christ Church Bell
And many a lesser bell *sound* through the room

In each of these three examples, the tenses indicate one action or condition as taking place or beginning *before* another, thus establishing a sequence. The perfect tense in each case (formed with *have*) reaches back to describe a time prior to the one described by the other, simple, tense. The verbs can be listed accordingly:

Prior action	*Later action*
had deepened	*in the past*: groped
has come	*in the present*: sound
shall have written	*in the future*: [shall be]

Within the sequences established by the narrative use of tense, the times of the verbal actions are presented as *definite*. That is, there is a claim made for the actions occurring at definite times, just as with a definite determiner there is the claim of a definite identity for the item referred to. In the tense system, the definiteness depends upon the fact that the present tense, in a narrative sequence, always coincides with the moment in the discourse when it occurs. When the discourse indicates its own moment of realisation (as it does through the present tense), that moment is as definite as the very fact of there being a discourse. Since all the other narrative tenses establish their references in relation to this 'present' moment, those tenses may be said to indicate definite times for the occurrences of their actions, too. ('Definite' does not necessarily mean 'instantaneous'.)

In the past and present sequences, there are other forms besides the simple past and present (as in 'groped' and 'sound') for representing the event closer to the moment of use in the discourse. To alter the examples, there are the following:

(4) When night had deepened,
I *was groping* my way from beech to hazel wood
(5) Midnight has come, and the great Christ Church Bell
And many a lesser bell *are sounding* through the room

These forms, made with the verb *to be* and the present participle, stress the simultaneity of the two narrated actions. And, in the case of the present tense form, the actions are also stressed as being simultaneous with the moment of use in the discourse. Because of this emphasis on simultaneity (which leads back ultimately to the instance of use), these forms are felt to have a greater degree of definiteness than the corresponding simple tense forms. Although the simple forms acquire definiteness in narrative contexts, as in (3), they do not possess it intrinsically the way the forms with -*ing* do. As a matter of fact, while the past form with -*ed* is neutral or unmarked as to definiteness, the simple present is marked as being *indefinite*.

Since theoretically all the tenses used in narrative are definite, what seems to have been observed in comparing the simple forms with those using -*ing* is the influence of certain non-narrative meanings in tenses occurring in narrative. And this is the case. Non-narrative tenses, which are not used especially for placing events in a sequence, do exhibit the opposition between definite and indefinite indications. The two forms noted in (4) and (5) are identical with the definite past and definite present forms of the non-narrative tenses.

Non-narrative tenses have two main forms of the present, as in these examples:

(6) Beloved, gaze in thine own heart,
     The holy tree *is growing* there
(7) Love's pleasure *drives* his love away,
     The painter's brush *consumes* his dreams

The *definite* tense, in (6), refers to an action which is simultaneous (if not co-extensive) with a specific present moment, namely, the moment of use. The definiteness here is not very different from the narrative present of (5) above. In (7), however, the present tense apparently indicates that the action occurs generally and that it may not be occurring at the moment of discourse. This tense does not refer to a specific occasion and is thus *indefinite*.

The forms of the present and past tenses are as follows:

	Non-narrative Forms	
	Present	Past
Definite	is -ing	was -ing
Indefinite	(simple form, e.g., *walks*)	have -ed

The fact that the *is* -*ing* form is definite may be seen in the strangeness or incompatibility sensed when it occurs with indications of indefinite time. For example:

(8) He is reading on Mondays.

It sounds more natural to say 'He reads on Mondays', using the indefinite form of the verb. An interpretation by which (8) would seem natural – e.g., 'He is reading on Mondays now that the rest of the week is given over to classes' – would make 'on Mondays' an indicator not of indefinite time but of a time which is definite in contrast to another period ('the rest of the week').

The compatibility of the simple form of the verb 'reads' with the adverbial of indefinite time shows the indefinite meaning carried by that verb form:

(9) He reads on Mondays.[3]

A further test would be to place the verb in a context with a definite time marker and see if awkwardness results:

(10) He reads at this moment.[4]

It is clearly more usual to have the definite form:

(11) He is reading at this moment.

Examples of the past tenses may also be tested in an adverbial context:

(12) He was reading on Monday.
(13) He has read on Monday.

The different meanings given to the same adverbial bring out the indefinite/definite opposition. The verb in (12) is apparently definite, since the adverbial there clearly refers to a specific Monday. With (13), indefiniteness is brought out: 'Monday' is not felt to refer to a specific day but rather to any number of Mondays.

The indefinite past in an example like (13) differs from the definite, narrative use of the same form (*have* -*ed*), the use seen in example (3). In narrative, the form is used along with present tenses to describe definite actions which have just taken place. In non-narrative use, the form describes actions which have taken place at an indefinite time in the past. These examples illustrate the definite and indefinite uses respectively:

(14) He *has come* into the room. Now he is walking toward the chair.
(15) He often *has come* into the room.

It can be seen that the non-narrative system of tenses differs from the narrative system mainly in having an indefinite dimension. The indefinite dimension is realised in the simple form of the verb (e.g., 'reads') and in the form with *has/have* plus *-ed*. The non-narrative definite forms (with *-ing*) are virtually equivalent to the same forms as they appear in narrative sequences.

The masks of tense come about through a use of the *indefinite* present tense form in contexts where one normally would expect the *definite* form (either narrative or non-narrative).[5] This use pervades Yeats's text, creating masks in poem after poem. What happens in this use is that the indefinite form can no longer remain strictly indefinite. But neither can it become completely definite, as a positive indicator that the action coincides with a moment of use. The form instead becomes a mask. It becomes ambiguous as to definiteness and indefiniteness and undecidable as to its time indication. For example:

(16) The unpurged images of day *recede*;
     The Emperor's drunken soldiery are abed

From the outset (and these lines begin the poem) the context is a definite one. The subject of the verb 'recede' is presented as fully identified (by cataphoric reference to one or more modifiers). And, with the second line, the definiteness of the description is reinforced. The indefinite present seems to have the same sort of awkwardness here as was felt in example (10). What would be expected in this context would be the definite present tense – 'are receding' – which would indicate a definite moment for the action. The tense as given seems somehow in relation to such a moment without being able to fix its action there.

The contexts in the following examples similarly demand the definite present – though in Yeats the indefinite is used.[6] Frequently the contexts set up a narrative, and there the definite tense would be the more usual one. Definite determiners and adverbials are also frequent. Non-restrictive sentence modifiers also occur, such as 'Raging at his own image . . .' in example (17). These, like non-restrictive relative clauses, usually modify something felt to be known and, at least to some degree, definite.

(17) The peahens *dance* on a smooth lawn,
      A parrot *sways* upon a tree,
      Raging at his own image in the enamelled sea
(18) The dews *drop* slowly and dreams *gather*. . . .
      We who still *labour* by the cromlech on the shore,[7]
      The grey cairn on the hill, when day *sinks* drowned in dew,
      Being weary of the world's empires, *bow* down to you
(19) The old brown thorn-trees *break* in two high over Cummen Strand,
      Under a bitter black wind that *blows* from the left hand
(20) O hurry where by water among the trees
      The delicate-stepping stag and his lady *sigh*
(21) The trees are in their autumn beauty,
      The woodland paths are dry,
      Under the October twilight the water
      Mirrors a still sky
(22) But now they *drift* on the still water
(23) With the old kindness, the old distinguished grace,
      She *lies*, her lovely piteous head amid dull red hair
      Propped upon pillows
(24) Under your old wind-beaten tower, where still
      A lamp *burns* on beside the open book
      That Michael Robartes left, you *walk* in the moon
(25) Minnaloushe *runs* in the grass
      Lifting his delicate feet
(26) all about it
      Reel shadows of the indignant desert birds.
      The darkness *drops* again . . .
      And what rough beast, its hour come round at last,
      Slouches towards Bethlehem to be born?
(27) But now wind *drops*, dust *settles*; thereupon
      There *lurches* past, his great eyes without thought . . .
      That insolent fiend Robert Artisson

(28) her nape caught in his bill,
      He *holds* her helpless breast upon his breast
(29) And thereupon my heart is driven wild:
      She *stands* before me as a living child
(30) At midnight on the Emperor's pavement *flit*
      Flames that no faggot *feeds*, nor steel has lit
(31) Bolt and bar the shutter/For the foul winds *blow*
(32) Bland Rhadamanthus *beckons* him . . .
      Salt blood *blocks* his eyes
(33) On all the tragic scene they *stare*.
      One *asks* for mournful melodies;
      Accomplished fingers *begin* to play
(34) Those Innocents *re-live* their death,
      Their wounds *open* again.
      The ecstatic waters *laugh* . . .
      And the brute dolphins *plunge*
(35) His hand *moves* to and fro.
      Like a long-legged fly upon the stream
      His mind *moves* upon silence.

These examples show the peculiar time dimension of the verbal mask, a dimension, consisting of a perpetual differentiation (apparently between definiteness and indefiniteness) within a 'present' time. The time of the action in each example seems to be both approaching and retreating from a present definite instant, but further characteristics of the indefinite and definite presents figure in this paradoxical movement.

The definiteness of present tense forms with *-ing* emphasises the simultaneity of the moment of action and the moment in the discourse when the verb occurs. The action denoted by the verb is presented as happening at the same time as the occurrence of the verb. There is an intrinsic connection between this tense form and the concept of 'now' or the 'present'. But the definite present is employed not merely because the action it describes happens to coincide with the time of the discourse. This tense is employed because there is a need to *bring out* the 'nowness' of the action. (The locutor could always choose to wait, and describe the action in the past tense.)

Under what circumstances would the fact that an action is happening 'now' need to be focused upon and when could it be taken for granted? If the participants in a discourse witnessing together an action or series of actions, each will be aware not only of the action but also of the other's simultaneous awareness of it. The 'nowness' of the action would probably be taken for granted. And in discussing the action – that is, the undoubtedly shared aspects of it – the participants could have no need to bring out its 'nowness' by using the definite present tense. It is the speaker's decision whether or not to present an action as shared – even one taking place before the eyes of both speaker and hearer. The speaker also has the option of omitting any focus on the presentness of the action. This option may be realised by using the indefinite present tense. An example might be the following statement, made when all participants seem to be aware of the action referred to – the approach of someone known to all:

(36)   Here comes Smith.

When there is a shared awareness of this sort between locutor and allocutor, the item so presented may be said to be a 'given' of the discourse. It is presented as something assumed to be known to all participants. If, on the other hand, the locutor notices something that he or she thinks the allocutor may *not* be aware of, it can be emphasised as a 'new' item in the discourse.[8] A new item may be marked as new in various ways. In the case of an action or anything else referred to by a verb, what is usually found is the definite present tense. For example:

(37)   Look, Smith is coming.

Here, the emphatic claim that the information is new is analogous to the mode of operation of the situational demonstratives. With both, there is an attempt to forge a nexus between the allocutor's attention and the item being introduced into the discourse.[9]

An extreme example of this kind of discourse – where there is an almost constant need to use the definite present – occurs when a sequence of events is being carried out by the locutor in a remote location and is being simultaneousy narrated (and somehow transmitted) to an allocutor:

(38)   I am entering the room. Now I am walking
         toward the . . .

The same tense prevails when such a sequence is being observed and narrated by the locutor:

(39)   He is entering the room. Now he is walking
       toward the . . .

In these cases, there is no opportunity for the allocutor to share the locutor's awareness of an action other than through the discourse. So every item must carry the emphasis of something new and be so marked by means of the definite present tense.

The indefinite present, by contrast, will occur only where there is no need to emphasise either the newness or the presentness of the action, where for one reason or another the action is given. Besides the common situation of shared awareness, as described above, there are a number of circumstances where this is typically the case. If, for example, someone wishes to narrate a series of non-present actions in a dramatic way, describing, and perhaps demonstrating, how the series is to be carried out in some future situation, the indefinite present might be used as follows:

(40)   Smith waits here until the door opens, then he
       immediately moves to the far end of the room.

This use is related to the so-called 'historical present', which may be thought of as a dramatisation in the present of obviously past actions. In both uses, the context makes it clear that the actions are not present ones. There is no attempt, as there would be were the definite present used, to give the actions other than an illusory or dramatised presentness. In another use of the indefinite present, the actions *are* present, but there is still no need to focus on that fact. The actions are performed (by the locutor in the presence of the allocutor) at the same time as they are described.[10] An example might occur in the demonstration of a piece of equipment (such sentences usually have the pronoun 'I' as subject):

(41)   I grasp the handle and turn it thus.

If the allocutor sees the action taking place as the locutor is performing it, the fact that it is taking place in the present need not be focused upon.[11]

The indefinite present thus subsists in a present which it

perpetually avoids. It avoids an emphatic connection to the 'now' and indicates its actions as 'given'. It places its actions in the dimension of the 'already'. But what seems to happen is that this dimension is constantly returning to the 'now' necessary to it. So the indefinite present can never permanently avoid the kind of presentness characteristic of the definite tense. The indefinite, then, is split. It is intrinsically double. In the examples cited above there was an intensification of its doubleness – and consequently an intensification of the mask – brought about by the indefinite's occurring in definite contexts.

So, the time of the mask can be described as a differential series, for it is founded on a tense differing from itself. In the examples from Yeats there is a repeated approach toward and retreat from a present – a movement which seems to be due to the doubleness of the the tense. This movement is what defines the dimension of the maskevent. The tense seems perpetually to propagate and then displace its present instant. The definite dimension of this present repeatedly cuts into or traverses the indefinite dimensions. So the present time of the mask perpetually moves but does not change as to its presentness.

As the process of antiplatonisation begins to subvert the ability of language to represent time as a sequential flow, language and literature themselves start to move within a differential sort of time. Time, as in the mask, becomes purely a function of the event as an instantaneously 'present' but repetitious entity. The event is the only thing felt any longer to be in contact with time, but the event, like the mask, is differential. Modern writing will persistently try to capture events, by dramatising them, tracking down their origins and interpreting them – but always with a sense of their elusiveness and absence. Both time and events, as we see from the syntactic masks' peculiar way of taking place, seem to escape every thought of absolute knowledge.

Appendix: Sources of Examples from Yeats

The list below identifies the source of each numbered example, the example number being followed by the number of the page in the *Variorum Edition* where the example occurs.

INTRODUCTION

1 – 136
2 – 287
3 – 324
4 – 324
5 – 338
6 – 346
7 – 411
8 – 481
9 – 549
10 – 353
11 – 380
12 – 423
13 – 435

CHAPTER 1

1 – 447–8
2 – 443
3 – 438
4 – 119
5 – 291
6 – 311
7 – 403
8 – 513
9 – 523
10 – 523
11 – 617
12 – 409
13 – 322
14 – 322
15 – 415
16 – 424
17 – 425
18 – 427
19 – 470
20 – 490
21 – 618
22 – 372
23 – 373
24 – 385
25 – 358
26 – 410
27 – 631
28 – 406
29 – 393
30 – 105
31 – 351
32 – 321
33 – 369
34 – 406
35 – 536
36 – 619
37 – 623
38 – 637
39 – 449
40 – 440
41 – 365–6
42 – 407
43 – 498
44 – 134–5
45 – 428, 430
46 – 431
47 – 441
48 – 443
49 – 500
50 – 407
51 – 322
52 – 442
53 – 504

CHAPTER 2

1 – 324
2 – 347

CHAPTER 2 (Contd.)

3 – 368	43 – 344	84 – 501
4 – 401	44 – 344	85 – 559
5 – 418	45 – 316	86 – 564
6 – 446	46 – 559	87 – 338
7 – 514	47 – 379	88 – 405
8 – 150	48 – 389	89 – 476
9 – 264	49 – 480	90 – 300
10 – 291	50 – 535	91 – 365
11 – 318	51 – 135	92 – 65
12 – 326	52 – 490	93 – 368
13 – 344	53 – 490	94 – 336
14 – 347	54 – 401	95 – 110
15 – 347	55 – 441	96 – 149
16 – 369	56 – 441	97 – 294
17 – 382	57 – 441	98 – 378
18 – 403	58 – 441	99 – 379
19 – 405	59 – 441	100 – 437
20 – 408	60 – 441	101 – 445
21 – 408	61 – 441	102 – 445
22 – 427	62 – 441	103 – 531
23 – 430	63 – 422	104 – 611
24 – 441	64 – 386	105 – 455
25 – 442	65 – 393	106 – 455
26 – 472	66 – 399	107 – 509
27 – 477	67 – 400	108 – 512
28 – 497	68 – 402	109 – 524
29 – 630	69 – 403	110 – 530
30 – 610	70 – 406	111 – 638
31 – 441	71 – 321	112 – 638
32 – 437	72 – 407	113 – 640
33 – 322	73 – 409	114 – 427
34 – 442	74 – 416	115 – 138
35 – 504	75 – 416	116 – 174
36 – 112	76 – 418	117 – 254
37 – 119	77 – 427	118 – 318
38 – 123	78 – 436	119 – 344
39 – 158	79 – 442	120 – 399
40 – 164	80 – 446	121 – 414
41 – 325	81 – 473	122 – 421
42 – 344	82 – 481	123 – 434
	83 – 482	124 – 435

125–440
126–444
127–452
128–484
129–497
130–498
131–530
132–630
133–259
134–293
135–315
136–345
137–445
138–533
139–537
140–438
141–162
142–345
143–498
144–495
145–476
146–481
147–501
148–383
149–637
150–444
151–409
152–411
153–478
154–483
155–490
156–501
157–639

CHAPTER 3

1–411
2–622
3––
4––

5–320
6–117
7–411
8––
9–209
10–353
11–92
12–92
13–210
14–272
15–371
16–209
17–330
18–66
19–101
20–136
21–298
22–320
23–369
24–587
25–630
26––
27–349
28––
29–349
30–78
31–88
32–260
33–165
34–301
35–316
36–198
37–262
38–326
39–344
40–345
41–399
42–414
43–428
44–483
45–538

46–510
47–640
48–445
49––
50––
51––
52––
53––
54––

CHAPTER 4

1–199
2–320
3–314
4–363
5–398
6–406
7–405
8–416
9–446
10–477
11–478
12–617
13–381
14–415
15–438
16–356
17––
18–612
19–348
20–348
21–517
22–206
23–176
24–351
25–442
26–501
27–125–6
28–149

Appendix

CHAPTER 4 (*Contd.*)
29 – 330
30 – 324
31 – 371
32 – 443-4
33 – 176
34 – 327
35 – 343
36 – 364
37 – 441
38 – 477
39 – 498
40 – 537
41 – 629
42 – 629
43 – 161
44 – 177
45 – 318
46 – 322-3
47 – 257
48 – 325
49 – 370
50 – 410
51 – 320-1
52 – 321
53 – 320
54 – 321
55 – 321
56 – 321

CHAPTER 5

1 – 283
2 – 348
3 – 470
4 – —
5 – —
6 – 134
7 – 438
8 – —
9 – —
10 – —
11 – —
12 – —
13 – —
14 – —
15 – —
16 – 497
17 – 77
18 – 161
19 – 206
20 – 210
21 – 322
22 – 323
23 – 362
24 – 367
25 – 378
26 – 402
27 – 433
28 – 441
29 – 444
30 – 498
31 – 523
32 – 530
33 – 567
34 – 612
35 – 618
36 – —
37 – —
38 – —
39 – —
40 – —
41 – —

Notes

INTRODUCTION: THE SYNTACTIC MASKS

1. Discussion has been initiated mainly by the so-called 'post-structuralists' – such figures as Sollers, Kristeva, Barthes, Derrida, Foucault and Deleuze – those French writers, critics and philosophers who have been grouped together (by observers of the critical scene) largely because of their interest in these very aspects of modern writing and thought.
2. The term is used in the same sense in G. Deleuze, *Différence et répétition* and *Logique du sens*. Deleuze's conception of antiplatonism is usefully discussed in M. Foucault, 'Theatrum philosophicum'. In philosophy, a decisive moment for the shift in subjectivity was the Kantian analysis of Descartes' cogito as a subject that merely accompanies thoughts or judgments as an empty vehicle for predicates: 'The "I" is indeed in all thoughts, but there is not in this representation the least trace of intuition. . . . Beyond this logical meaning of the "I", we have no knowledge of the subject in itself, which as substratum underlies this "I", as it does all thoughts. . . . The unity of consciousness, which underlies the categories, is here mistaken for an intuition of the subject as object, and the category of substance is then applied to it' (Kant, *Critique of Pure Reason*, 334, 377). Crucial for modern philosophical elaborations of the concept of difference was Hegel's (ostensibly idealist) logic, particularly his analysis of 'mediation' and 'negation'. See G. W. F. Hegel, 'La science de la logique', *Encyclopédie des sciences philosophiques en abrégé*.
3. The raw data for this study was obtained by a sentence by sentence syntactic analysis of over eighty percent of the total number of Yeats's poems.
4. L. Spitzer, *Linguistics and Literary History*, 14.
5. L. Spitzer, *Linguistics and Literary History*, 28.
6. R. Jakobson, 'Closing Statement: Linguistics and Poetics', 358. Elsewhere in the same article (p. 368), Jakobson writes: 'Briefly, equivalence in sound, projected into the sequence as its constitutive principle, inevitably involves semantic equivalence . . .'.
7. See note 1 above and Selected Bibliography. All of the mentioned writers can be read practically at random for their positions toward language and meaning. For a collection including all the mentioned writers (except Deleuze), see *Théorie d'ensemble* (1968).
8. The relative clause is discussed in more detail in Chapter 3.
9. All quotations from Yeats's poetry are from the *Variorum Edition*. Examples are numbered (consecutively within each chapter) for ease of reference. The Appendix lists the page in the *Variorum* where each example may be found.
10. This non-standard usage is a feature of the Anglo-Irish dialect, which as Yeats said 'gets from Gaelic its syntax and keeps its still partly Tudor vocabulary'.

Anglo-Irish tends to use a single form of the relative pronoun, i.e., *that*, in every context perhaps because Gaelic does the same. The Gaelic relative particle (with a base form *a*) does not carry information as to whether or not the antecedent is a person (unlike English *who/which*), nor does it distinguish between subject and object (unlike English *who/whom*). Similarly, *that* is the most unmarked relative pronoun in English. Examples directly imitating Anglo-Irish speech can be found in Yeats's early plays, e.g.: 'Johnny Gibbons *that* is at this time an outlaw' (*Variorum Edition of the Plays*, 652). The form is frequent in Lady Gregory's translations from Gaelic, e.g.: 'Ferceirtne, *that* was very learned, and Morann, *that* could not give a wrong judgment' (*Cuchulain of Muirthemne*, 51–2). The use of *that*, discussed here in non-restrictives, is also pervasive in Yeats as a personal subject (as opposed to the object) in restrictives: 'I'll name the friends *that* cannot sup with us'; 'A girl *that* knew all Dante once'; 'Old merchant skipper *that* leaped overboard'. R. Quirk ('Relative Clauses in Educated Spoken English', 107) notes that *who* 'is the overwhelmingly preferred pronoun where it is subject in a clause relating to a personal antecedent'.

11. F. de Saussure, *Cours de linguistique générale*, 166.
12. G. Deleuze, *Logique du sens*, 302.
13. Deleuze discusses Bergson as a source of this idea. For a discussion of memory and subjectivity as contraction, see H. Bergson, *Matière et mémoire*. Of memory, Bergson writes: 'Coextensive à la conscience, elle retient et aligne à la suite les uns des autres tous nos états.... Dans la perception concrète la mémoire intervient, et la subjectivité des qualités sensibles tient justement à ce que notre conscience, qui commence par n'être que mémoire, prolonge les uns dans les autres, pour les contracter dans une intuition unique, une pluralité de moments' (168, 246). (Coextensive with consciousness, it retains and aligns all our states in sequence.... Memory intervenes in concrete perception, and the subjectivity of perceptible qualities depends precisely on the fact that our consciousness, which begins by being nothing but memory, extends some of them into others so as to contract a plurality of moments into a single intuition.)
14. W. B. Yeats, *Mythologies*, 365–6.
15. Discussing the Four Faculties, Yeats writes: 'The being becomes conscious of itself as a separate being, because of certain facts of Opposition and Discord, the emotional Opposition of *Will* and *Mask*, the intellectual Opposition of *Creative Mind* and *Body of Fate*, Discords between *Will* and *Creative Mind*, *Creative Mind* and *Mask*, *Mask* and *Body of Fate*, *Body of Fate* and *Will*'. (*A Vision*, 93).
16. As a self-enclosed entity, the work had to fall back on its inner dynamics, the operation of which tended to be described in formalist terms. Ideally, the work was to become as organically integrated as the mind itself – as Coleridge put it, 'diverging and contracting with the same activity of the assimilative and of the modifying faculties' and showing 'the balance or reconciliation of opposite or discordant qualities'. (S. T. Coleridge, *Biographia Literaria*, 180, 174.)
17. Mallarmé wrote: 'L'oeuvre pure implique la disparition élocutoire du poëte, qui cède l'initiative aux mots, par le heurt de leur inégalité mobilisés' ('Crise de vers', *Oeuvres complètes*, 366). (The pure work implies the disappearance as speaker of the poet, who cedes the initiative to the words, mobilised by the shock of their difference.) Cf. Yeats on his own early work: 'an art as separate from everything heterogeneous and casual, from all character and circumstance, as some Herodiade ... dancing seemingly alone in her narrow moving

luminous circle' (*Autobiography*, 193).
18. For a discussion of the mask in relation to modern conceptions of the self in art, see L. Trilling, *Sincerity and Authenticity*, esp. 106–33.
19. O. Wilde, 'Epigrams', in *The Works of Oscar Wilde*, vol. 11, 106. (Quoted in Trilling, *Sincerity and Authenticity*.) See also, Wilde's essays, e.g., 'The Truth of Masks: A Note on Illusion', where he wrote: 'A Truth in art is that whose contradiction is also true' (*The Works of Oscar Wilde*, vol. 9, 238). The notion of the higher truth of artifice is important in romantic aesthetics. Cf. Schiller: 'man only plays when in the full meaning of the word he is a man, and he is only completely a man when he plays' ('Letters Upon the Aesthetical Education of Man', Letter XV, *Essays Aesthetical and Philosophical*, 71).
20. Foucault provides a full discussion of this shift in linguistic models that took place from the 'classical age' to the 19th and 20th centuries. See *Les mots et les choses*, especially 32–136, 245–9, 292–313.
21. The linguist E. Benveniste (though still with a platonic view of the subject) has described this tendency: 'Le langage n'est possible que parce que chaque locuteur se pose comme *sujet*, en renvoyant à lui-même comme *je* dans son discours. De ce fait, *je* pose une autre personne, celle qui, tout extérieure qu'elle est à "moi", devient mon écho auquel je dis *tu* et qui me dit *tu*. La polarité des personnes, telle est dans le langage la condition fondamentale, dont le procès de communication, dont nous sommes parti, n'est qu'une conséquence toute pragmatique' ('De la subjectivité dans le langage', *Problèmes de linguistique générale*, 260). (Language is possible only because each speaker sets himself up as *subject*, by referring to himself as *I* in his discourse. From this fact, *I* set up another person, the one who, being completely exterior to 'me', becomes my echo to whom I say *you* and who says *you* to me. This polarity of persons is the fundamental condition of language, of which the process of communication is only a purely pragmatic consequence.)

CHAPTER 1: THE NOUN PHRASE AND THE DETERMINER

1. Usage varies as to what the determiner category is called; 'deictics' and 'determiners' are both used. But some mean by the latter everything that precedes the adjective – including the quantifier (e.g., 'all the . . .'). Here, 'determiner' will be used in the narrower sense to include only those items, like the articles, which have the same potential positions in the noun phrase as the articles. The term 'noun phrase' refers to the noun plus all its modifiers and other adjuncts, or any segment that can function like a noun in a sentence. The noun phrase contains at least the noun itself preceded by an article or other determiner. Modifiers may occur next to the noun – adjectives usually before, relative clauses after. A special type of modifier, the quantifier or pre-article, when it is present, occurs before the determiner (e.g., '*all* the golden codgers').
2. 'Allocutor' and other special terms are defined in the Glossary. For a discussion of 'allocutor' and 'locutor', see T. Todorov, 'Problèmes de l'énonciation', 4.
3. R. Jacobs and P. Rosenbaum (*English Transformational Grammar*, 44–5) include the 'demonstrative article' in this category. B. Strang (*Modern English Structure*, 128) calls the possessive pronoun so used the 'genitive article'.
4. The word *some* is sometimes considered a plural indefinite article. See

P. Roberts, *English Syntax*, 11–12. *Some* is a quantifier which fits into the determiner system and is used almost like 'null' with plural nouns. It emphasises the partial aspect of the entity following as compared with the whole class, as in *some books*. Another, quite distinct, use of *some* differs from the indefinite article use in that it occurs with singular nouns and has a stronger stress (just as the demonstrative article has a stronger stress than *the*). This *some* (which has been called the 'nondefinite demonstrative'; see Roberts, 32–3) is notable in Yeats; for example: 'Some green wing' and 'Surely some revelation is at hand'. The demonstrative *some* can also stand alone as a pronoun: e.g., 'Some burn damp faggots'.
5. The 'situational' use corresponds to the familiar 'pointing' or properly 'demonstrative' use of demonstratives. But since demonstratives have other functions as well, the separate term 'situational' is useful. And it can be applied to the related use of *the*. See M. Halliday, 'Notes on Transitivity and Theme in English', Part 2, 231–6. The posessives can also have a 'situational' use, if they call attention to the presence of the possessor: 'It's *her* book'.
6. In the context of 'The Resurrection', from which 'Two Songs from a Play' are taken, the noun phrase 'that room' has an explicit antecedent, so the use of 'that' would be anaphoric there.
7. Often there are also indirect clues that help to establish the situation, such as 'there', 'Under my window-ledge', and 'Here'. Many times the situation is suggested by the titles of poems or volumes, e.g., *The Wild Swans at Coole* and *The Tower*. Poems will provide contexts for other poems; for example, the whole series with the tower as setting, beginning with 'In Memory of Major Robert Gregory' and including 'To be carved on a stone at Thoor Ballylee'. The series also includes: 'Ego Dominus Tuus', 'A Prayer on going into my House', 'The Phases of the Moon', 'A Prayer for my Daughter', 'The Tower', 'Meditations in Time of Civil War', 'A Dialogue of Self and Soul', and 'Blood and the Moon'.
8. When the modifiers fully effect the identification, the noun phrase can no longer be said to be identified anaphorically. When the identifying element is located in the modifier, the reference, to use Halliday's terminology, is 'cataphoric'. Halliday ('Notes', Part 2, 231) observes that the reference of demonstratives 'may be either situational . . . or textual, and if textual may be either backward (anaphoric) or forward (cataphoric)'. Cataphoric identification is discussed in the next chapter.
9. The second relative clause could be taken as non-restrictive or non-defining. The two types of relative clause and their behaviour in cases like this are discussed in Chapter 3.
10. The lines are ambiguous in that 'furies', 'images', and 'sea' may also be read as a series of direct objects of 'Break'. But the likelihood that the latter two are in apposition and characterise the 'furies of complexity' is reinforced at various points – for example, in the line: 'Spirit after spirit! The smithies break the flood', where the spirits are perhaps another term for both 'furies' and 'images'.

CHAPTER 2: THE NOUN PHRASE AND THE MODIFIER

1. See Halliday, 'Descriptive Linguistics in Literary Studies'.
2. Transformational grammar derives most adjectival and phrasal modifiers from

relative clauses: transformations delete the relative pronoun and the copula, and, if what remains is a single-word adjective, it is moved in front of the noun. Thus, 'the wintry blast' would be said to come from a remote structure 'the blast [which is] wintry' and 'the apple on the bough' from 'the apple [which is] on the bough'. If the adjective has a phrasal complement, the entire modifier follows the noun, as in 'gravity/ Appropriate to that beating breast'. Traditional poeticisms often have single-word adjectives after nouns (e.g., 'old thorns innumerable'; 'a seat/ Chryselephantine'). Compared adjective constructions either wholly or partially follow the noun (e.g., 'A voice/ Soft as the rustle of a reed'; 'A more dream-heavy hour than this'). A modifier consisting of a participle and another element such as a prepositional phrase is another common type of reduced relative clause (e.g., 'Hades' bobbin bound in mummy-cloth').

3. This is related to the fact that more than one restrictive relative clause may modify a noun. See C. Smith, 'Determiners and Relative Clauses in a Generative Grammar of English', 42.
4. For a discussion of this mechanism (and of the relation of *the* to the noun phrase and its modes of identification), see M. Halliday, 'Descriptive Linguistics in Literary Studies' and 'The Linguistic Study of Literary Texts'.
5. Although it is possible to find a noun and its modifiers exactly copied as a unit in an anaphoric second mention, it is rare. An example in Yeats, with a relative clause modifier: 'There was a man whom Sorrow named his friend . . . / And then the man whom Sorrow named his friend/ Cried out . . . / And then the man whom Sorrow named his friend/ Sought once again the shore . . .' ('The Sad Shepherd', *Variorum Edition*, 67–8).
6. *This* is more frequently cataphoric. See Halliday, 'Notes', Part 2, 232. In situational references, modifiers may aid the demonstratives in effecting identification (e.g., 'That green book belongs to me').
7. Halliday, 'Descriptive Linguistics in Literary Studies'. The following discussion essentially presents Halliday's view of the poem. But the analysis of the anaphoric noun phrases differs from Halliday's. For (55), Halliday includes the next words 'beating still . . .' as a postnominal modifier (or 'qualifier'). In addition, he considers the structure in the next line, 'her thighs caressed . . .', a modified anaphoric noun phrase because, again, he counts 'caressed . . .' as a postnominal modifier. But (55) belongs in our discussion of modified anaphoric noun phrases only by virtue of 'great' – and 'her thighs caressed' not at all. The participles 'beating' and 'caressed' (as well as 'caught' in the next line) form *nominative absolute* constructions with the preceding nouns. In absolutes, which have been analysed as coming from independent sentences, the function of the participial phrase is always to predicate something about the noun phrase and never to define it. Halliday also includes the 'beating' that follows (59) as a postnominal modifier, whereas it clearly functions as a 'verb phrase complement' – parallel to 'sing' in the sentence 'I heard her sing'. See P. Rosenbaum, *The Grammar of English Predicate Complement Constructions*, 28.
8. The noun phrases containing two of these kinetic participles, 'the staggering girl' and 'her loosening thighs', contain anapests. Along with three other such feet, they serve to break up the otherwise solidly iambic structure of the poem. See J. Unterecker, *A Reader's Guide to William Butler Yeats*, 189.
9. In normal speech, the tense of the main verbs 'holds' and 'engenders' does not

convey present action, but something habitual. This tense form, an important feature of Yeats's poetry, is discussed in Chapter 5.
10. J. Kristeva, 'Sémanalyse et production du sens: quelques problèmes de sémiotique littéraire à propos d'un texte de Mallarmé: *Un coup de dés*', 227.
11. It also seems to have a generic meaning, like the nouns in Wordsworth's lines: 'Never did *sun* more beautifully steep/ In his first splendour, *valley, rock*, or *hill*'.
12. In early drafts – 'the oblivious honey' and 'the generative honey' – example (150) did not have a conflict between 'null' and its (then adjectival) modifiers. These versions are given in T. Parkinson, *W. B. Yeats: The Later Poetry*, 98.

CHAPTER 3: THE RELATIVE CLAUSE

1. The branches, splitting the parts into increasingly particular elements, have been simplified for the sake of clarity. But they could show further particularisation, analysing the verb phrases and the relative clauses themselves, and including such elements as determiners and tense. The analysis of non-restrictive clauses follows R. Jacobs and P. Rosenbaum, *English Transformational Grammar*, 260–2.
2. R. Quirk ('Relative Clauses in Educated Spoken English', 101) describes these sound features: 'Restrictive clauses . . . are linked to their antecedents by close syntactic juncture, by unity of intonation contour, and by continuity of the degree of loudness. By contrast, non-restrictive clauses are characterized by open juncture, . . . a fresh intonation contour, and a change (especially a diminution) in the degree of loudness'.
3. M. Halliday, 'Notes on Transitivity and Theme in English', Part 2, 202.
4. Halliday, 'Notes', Part 2, 209.
5. Yeats wrote to Bridges: 'I do not understand stops. I write my work so completely for the ear that I feel helpless when I have to measure pauses by stops and commas' (*Letters*, 598). As Jon Stallworthy remarks (*Between the Lines*, 13), 'Punctuation . . . was frequently put in after the words were written, and put in as often by Mrs. Yeats, or the publisher, as by the poet himself'.
6. For a full discussion of the system of stress and non-stress in information units, see Halliday, 'Notes', Part 2, 199–244. For the grammatical consequences of pitch movement within this system, see 'Notes' as well as two other studies by Halliday: 'Intonation Systems in English' and *Intonation and Grammar in British English*.
7. Quirk, 'Relative Clauses in Educated Spoken English', 101.
8. See Introduction.
9. 'Where' seems most locative in (50), where 'blossoming' and 'dancing' are verbal; thus the words 'in the place where' could be substituted for the simple pronoun. The need for a location for action is not as great in (49), so 'where' tends to mean 'in instances where' or 'in cases where'. 'Wherever', 'when', or 'whenever' could also be substituted in (49).
10. The restrictive interpretation is reinforced by the absence of a comma before the pronoun, though with Yeats punctuation is not a firm guide.
11. Even with this use of 'or', the reading would allow the gerunds to be modified if the relative pronoun were a distributive pronoun, such as 'in either of which' or 'in both of which', rather than just 'where'. A remote possibility would have the clause modify only 'dancing'.

12. When a noun is followed by the verb *to be* (a predicating 'operator'), whether for the purposes of description or definition, the noun is presented as indefinite or undefined. It is the purpose of what follows the verb *to be* to make the preceding noun henceforward more definite. For this reason, a non-restrictive clause, which adds non-identifying information to a noun already known, cannot follow the predicating clause. To alter the current example for the sake of clarity: 'Labour is good, in which the body is not bruised to pleasure soul'. If this is carefully read as a non-restrictive, its awkwardness becomes apparent. If, however, the clause is embedded right after the noun, the structure becomes acceptable: 'Labour, in which the body is not bruised to pleasure soul, is good'.
13. A proof of the resistance is the fact that contexts come to mind more readily for 'a blossoming' or 'blossomings' than for 'dancing' or 'dancings'. R. Kirsner (personal communication to author) has observed that when gerunds become count nouns they frequently refer to the product of an action (e.g., 'writings') rather than the event itself. This shade of meaning, too, is felt more in 'blossomings' than in 'dancings'.

CHAPTER 4: ADDITIVE STRUCTURING

1. In transformational grammar, such modifiers would be derived from relative clauses.
2. Often with enjambment the separation caused by the line structure cannot have the same effect, because the divided elements have no important unity as segments by themselves; for example, when the first line ends with a preposition ('Fix every wandering thought upon/That quarter') or with a transitive verb ('all neglect/ Monuments of unageing intellect').
3. M. Halliday, 'Notes on Transitivity and Theme in English', Part 2, 201.
4. Though this line seems to contain only part of a verb phrase, it is nevertheless felt as a complete constituent because the separation, by preposing, of the direct object, line 7, is a grammatical device, not a result of the line structure. The type of noun phrase found in line 7, the 'noun phrase complement', has been analysed as a clause embedded in a noun phrase. See R. Jacobs and P. Rosenbaum, *English Transformational Grammar*, 164–5.
5. The lines generally coincide with these components: clausal structures – 1, 3, 4, 5, 9, 15, 16, 17, 18, 20, 24, 26, 27, 28, 29, 32, 33; verb phrases (including their adverbials) – 7, 12, 19, 36; participial phrases – 11, 13, 14, 23; prepositional phrases – 6, 21, 30, 31; noun phrases – 2, 8, 25, 34; nominative absolute – 10; relative clause – 22; heterogeneous – 35. The second line, 'There the silver dew', could be considered a clausal structure, except for its lacking the verb 'lay'.
6. The complement, though not strictly an independent component, is also given an additive quality by the line structure in much the same way that relative clauses are. The later line 'Climbing up to a place' is ambiguous in relation to this complement because it can be taken either as a complement of the verb 'Imagining' or as a participial modifier of 'a man'.
7. For the second line, the 'tied' reading happens to be the more 'correct' one; for the first line, the opposite is true.
8. Cf.: 'The water here is extremely cold,' followed by the comment: 'I've felt water as cold'.

9. Beginning a line, this clause will become a mask for the reasons discussed in Chapter 3 – where it is given as example (22).
10. The subordinate clause is introduced by the idiomatic quasi-conjunction 'seeing that'.

CHAPTER 5: THE GRAMMAR OF TIME IN THE MASK

1. For a detailed treatment of time and the event in the context of differential series, see G. Deleuze, *Logique du sens*. The present discussion is indebted to Deleuze's.
2. For this distinction, and for a linguistic analysis of English tense, see W. Diver, 'The Chronological System of the English Verb', 141–81. The analogous distinction for French is discussed in E. Benveniste, 'Les relations de temps dans le verbe français', *Problèmes de linguistique générale*, 237–50.
3. With the indefinite present, in the absence of the plural form 'Mondays', which enforces the sentence's interpretation as a general truth, the sense could be future: 'He reads on Monday' meaning 'He is to read on the coming Monday'.
4. The example, with a different verb, is Diver's. See Diver, 'Chronological System', 173.
5. The discussion to follow concentrates on the use of indefinite *present* forms. There is a corresponding use of indefinite *past* forms in Yeats, as in 'I *have heard* the pigeons of the Seven Woods/Make their faint thunder' and 'I *have looked* upon those brilliant creatures,/And now my heart is sore'.
6. In some of these examples, the sense of a 'general truth' or 'usual occurrence' may enter into the interpretation, but the definiteness of the context usually counteracts it. The indefinite present is used with a generic sense in such lines as 'Men dance on deathless feet' and 'Both nuns and mothers worship images'.
7. Before being revised, this line had the definite tense: 'We, who *are labouring* by the cromlech on the shore'.
8. For the distinction between 'given' and 'new' items, see M. Halliday, 'Notes on Transitivity and Theme in English', Part 2, 200–11.
9. The use of determiners often works along with tenses in marking items as 'given' or 'new'. Halliday states that 'what is referred to anaphorically is "given", while what is referred to situationally or cataphorically is "new"' ('Notes', Part 2, 231).
10. This contrasts directly with narration from a remote location, which must use the definite present. See examples (38) and (39).
11. A special action of this type has been analysed by J. Austin as the 'illocutionary act': the 'performance of an act *in* saying something as opposed to performance of an act *of* saying something' (*How to Do Things with Words*, 99–100). The act is carried out by the uttering of certain words in the appropriate circumstances, e.g.: 'I hereby deny that'. The indefinite present can be used because, with act and verb coinciding in time, there is no need to focus on that time as present. Certain sentences in Yeats, though not illocutionary acts, nevertheless resemble them: 'And I *declare* my faith:/I *mock* Plotinus' thought'; 'for I *avow*/Such devilish things exist'; 'I *summon* to the winding ancient stair'.

Selected Bibliography

Annear, Sandra, 'Relative Clauses and Conjunctions', in *Working Papers in Linguistics*, no. *1* (Columbus, Ohio: Department of Linguistics and Research Center in Computer and Information Sciences at Ohio State University, 1967).

Audouard, Xavier, 'Le simulacre', *Cahiers pour l'analyse*, no. 3 (1966) 57-72.

Auerbach, Erich, *Mimesis: The Representation of Reality in Western Literature*, trans. W. Trask (New York: Doubleday, Anchor Books, 1957).

Austin, J. L., *How to Do Things with Words*., 2nd edn, ed. J. O. Urmson and M. Sbisà (Cambridge, Mass.: Harvard University Press, 1975).

Bach, Emmon, 'Nouns and Noun Phrases', in *Universals in Linguistic Theory*, ed. E. Bach and R. T. Harms (New York: Holt, Rinehart & Winston, 1968).

Bach, Emmon, and Robert T. Harms, eds, *Universals in Linguistic Theory* (New York: Holt, Rinehart & Winston, 1968).

Bar-Hillel, Yehoshua, *Language and Information* (Reading, Mass.: Addison-Wesley, 1964).

Barthes, Roland, *Le degré zéro de l'écriture* (Paris: Seuil, 1953).

——, *Le plaisir du texte* (Paris: Seuil, 1973).

Benveniste, Emile, 'L'appareil formel de l'énonciation', *Langages*, no. 17 (1960) 12-18; repr. in *Problèmes de linguistique générale, II* (Paris: Gallimard, 1974).

——, *Problèmes de linguistique générale* (Paris: Gallimard, 1966).

——, *Problèmes de linguistique générale, II* (Paris: Gallimard, 1974).

Bergson, Henri, *Essai sur les données immédiates de la conscience*, 154th edn (Paris: Presses Universitaires de France, 1976).

——, *L'évolution créatrice*, 30th edn (Paris: Alcan, 1926).

——, *Matière et mémoire*, 92nd edn (Paris: Presses Universitaires de France, 1968).

Blanchot, Maurice, *L'entretien infini* (Paris: Gallimard, 1969).

——, *L'espace littéraire* (Paris: Gallimard, 1955).

Blanchot, Maurice, *Le livre à venir* (Paris: Gallimard, 1959).
——, *La part du feu* (Paris: Gallimard, 1949).
Bloom, Harold, *Yeats* (New York: Oxford University Press, 1970).
Bowers, John, 'Adjectives and Adverbs in English', mimeograph (Bloomington, Indiana: Indiana University Linguistics Club, 1970).
Carnap, Rudolf, *The Logical Syntax of Language*, trans. A. Smeaton (London: Routledge & Kegan Paul, 1937).
Chomsky, Noam, *Aspects of the Theory of Syntax* (Cambridge, Mass.: MIT Press, 1965).
——, 'Remarks on Nominalization', mimeograph (Bloomington, Indiana: Indiana University Linguistics Club, 1968); repr. in *Studies on Semantics in Generative Grammar* (The Hague: Mouton, 1972).
——, *Studies on Semantics in Generative Grammar* (The Hague: Mouton, 1972).
——, *Syntactic Structures* (The Hague: Mouton, 1957).
——, and Morris Halle, *The Sound Pattern of English* (New York: Harper & Row, 1968).
Coleridge, Samuel Taylor, *Biographia Literaria*, ed. G. Watson (London: J. M. Dent, 1975).
Davidson, Donald, and Gilbert Harman, eds, *Semantics of Natural Language*, 2nd edn (Dordrecht: Reidel, 1972).
Deleuze, Gilles, 'A quoi reconnait-on le structuralisme?' in *Le XXe siècle*, by J. Bouveresse, *et al.* (Paris: Hachette, 1973).
——, *Le bergsonisme*, 2nd edn (Paris: Presses Universitaires de France, 1968).
——, 'La conception de la différence chez Bergson', *Les études bergsoniennes*, no. 4 (1956) 77–112.
——, 'Conclusions – sur la volonté de puissance et l'éternel retour', in *Nietzsche*, Cahiers de Royaumont, Philosophie, no. VI (Paris: Minuit, 1967).
——, *Différence et répétition* (Paris: Presses Universitaires de France, 1968).
——, *Logique du sens* (Paris: Minuit, 1969).
——, *Nietzsche et la philosophie* (Paris: Presses Universitaires de France, 1962).
de Man, Paul, 'Ludwig Binswanger et le problème du moi poétique', in *Les chemins actuels de la critique*, ed. G. Poulet (Paris: Union Générale d'Editions, '10/18', 1968).
——, 'Nietzsche's Theory of Rhetoric', *Symposium*, 28 (Spring 1974) 33–45.

Selected Bibliography

Derrida, Jacques, *De la grammatologie* (Paris: Minuit, 1967).
——, *La dissémination* (Paris: Seuil, 1972).
——, *L'écriture et la différence* (Paris: Seuil, 1967).
——, *Marges – de la philosophie* (Paris: Minuit, 1972).
——, 'Sémiologie et grammatologie', in *Essays in Semiotics*, ed. J. Kristeva, J. Rey–Debove, and D. J. Umiker (The Hague: Mouton, 1971).
——, *La voix et la phénomène* (Paris: Presses Universitaires de France, 1967).
Descartes, René, *Oeuvres et lettres*, ed. A. Bridoux (Paris: Gallimard, Bibliothèque de la Pléiade, 1953).
Diver, William, 'The Chronological System of the English Verb', *Word*, 19 (1963) 141–81.
Donato, Eugenio, 'Divine Agonies: of Representation and Narrative in Romantic Poetics', *Glyph*, no. 6 (1979) 90–122.
Ducrot, O., 'Les indéfinis et l'énonciation', *Langages*, no. 17 (1970) 91–111.
Eliot, T. S., *Selected Essays* (New York: Harcourt, Brace, 1950).
Ellmann, Richard, *The Identity of Yeats* (New York: Oxford University Press, Galaxy Books, 1964).
Fillmore, Charles J., and D. Terence Langendoen, eds, *Studies in Linguistic Semantics* (New York: Holt, Rinehart & Winston, 1971).
Fish, Stanley E., *Self-Consuming Artifacts* (Berkeley and Los Angeles: University of California Press, 1972).
Fodor, Jerry A., and Jerrold J, Katz, eds, *The Structure of Language: Readings in the Philosophy of Language* (Englewood Cliffs, New Jersey: Prentice-Hall, 1964).
Foucault, Michel, *L'archéologie du savoir* (Paris: Gallimard, 1969).
——, *Les mots et les choses: une archéologie des sciences humaines* (Paris: Gallimard, 1966).
——, *L'ordre du discours* (Paris: Gallimard, 1971).
——, 'Qu'est-ce qu'un auteur?', *Bulletin de la Société française de philosophie*, 64 (1969) 73–95.
——, 'Theatrum philosophicum', *Critique*, nos. 282 (1970) 885–908.
Frege, Gottlob, *Translations from the Philosophical Writings of Gottlob Frege*, ed. P. T. Geach and M. Black (Oxford: Basil Blackwell, 1970).
Geach, Peter T., *Reference and Generality*, emended edn (Ithaca: Cornell University Press, 1968).
Genette, Gérard, *Figures* (Paris: Seuil, 1966).

Genette, Gérard, *Figures II* (Paris: Seuil, 1969).
——, *Mimologiques: voyage en Cratylie* (Paris: Seuil, 1976).
Green, André, 'L'objet (a) de J. Lacan, sa logique et la théorie freudienne', *Cahiers pour l'analyse*, no. 3 (1966) 15–37.
Gregory, Augusta, *Cuchulain of Muirthemne*, 5th edn (New York: Oxford University Press, 1970).
Grinder, John, and Paul M. Postal, 'Missing Antecedents', *Linguistic Inquiry*, 2 (1971) 269–312.
Halliday, M. A. K., 'Descriptive Linguistics in Literary Studies', in *English Studies Today, Third Series*, ed. G. I. Duthie (Edinburgh: Edinburgh University Press, 1964); repr. in *Patterns of Language*, by M. A. K. Halliday and A. McIntosh (Bloomington, Indiana: Indiana University Press, 1966).
——, *Intonation and Grammar in British English* (The Hague: Mouton, 1967).
——, 'Intonation Systems in English', in *Patterns of Language*, by M. A. K. Halliday and A. McIntosh (Bloomington, Indiana: Indiana University Press, 1966).
——, 'The Linguistic Study of Literary Texts', in *Proceedings of the Ninth International Congress of Linguists*, ed. H. Lunt (The Hague: Mouton, 1964); repr. in *Essays on the Language of Literature*, ed. S. Chatman and S. R. Levin (Boston: Houghton Mifflin, 1967).
——, 'Notes on Transitivity and Theme in English', Parts 1 and 2: *Journal of Linguistics*, 3 (1967) 37–81, 199–244; Part 3: *Journal of Linguistics*, 4 (1968) 179–215.
Hartman, Geoffrey H., *Beyond Formalism: Literary Essays 1958–1970* (New Haven: Yale University Press, 1970).
——, *The Fate of Reading and Other Essays* (Chicago: University of Chicago Press, 1975).
Hegel, G. W. F., *Phenomenology of Spirit*, trans. A. V. Miller (New York: Oxford University Press, 1977).
——, *Encyclopédie des sciences philosophiques en abrégé*, trans M. de Gandillac (Paris: Gallimard, 1970).
Heidegger, Martin, *Nietzsche*: vol. 1: *The Will to Power as Art*, trans. D. F. Krell (San Francisco: Harper & Row, 1979).
Henn, T. R., *The Lonely Tower: Studies in the Poetry of W. B. Yeats*, 2nd edn (London: Methuen, 1965).
Hopkins, Gerard Manley, *The Journals and Papers of Gerard Manley Hopkins*, 2nd edn; ed. H. House, completed by G. Storey (London: Oxford University Press, 1959).
Irigaray, Luce, 'Le v(i)ol de la lettre', *Tel Quel*, no. 39 (1969) 64–77.

Jackendoff, Ray S., 'On Some Questionable Arguments About Quantifiers and Negation', mimeograph (Bloomington, Indiana: Indiana University Linguistics Club, 1970).

——, *Semantic Interpretation in Generative Grammar* (Cambridge, Mass.: MIT Press, 1972).

——, 'Speculations on Presentences and Determiners', mimeograph (Bloomington, Indiana: Indiana University Linguistics Club, 1968).

Jacobs, Roderick A., and Peter S. Rosenbaum., *English Transformational Grammar* (Waltham, Mass.: Blaisdell, 1968).

——, eds, *Readings in English Transformational Grammar* (Waltham, Mass.: Ginn, 1970).

Jakobson, Roman, 'Closing Statement: Linguistics and Poetics', in *Style in Language*, ed. T. A. Sebeok (Cambridge, Mass.: MIT Press, 1960).

——, *Essais de linguistique générale*, trans. N. Ruwet (Paris: Minuit, 1963).

——, 'Signe zéro', in *Mélanges de linguistique, offerts à Charles Bally* (Geneva: Georg, 1939); repr. in *Readings in Linguistics, II*, ed. E. P. Hamp, F. W. Householder and R. Austerlitz (Chicago: University of Chicago Press, 1966).

——, and Morris Halle, *Fundamentals of Language*, 2nd edn (The Hague: Mouton, 1971).

——, C. Gunnar M. Fant, and Morris Halle, *Preliminaries to Speech Analysis: the Distinctive Features and their Correlates*, 6th printing (Cambridge, Mass.: MIT Press, 1965).

Kant, Immanuel, *Critique of Pure Reason*, trans. N. K. Smith (London: Macmillan, 1933).

Karttunen, Lauri, 'Discourse Referents', mimeograph (Bloomington, Indiana: Indiana University Linguistics Club, 1971).

Katz, Jerrold J., and D. Terence Langendoen, 'Pragmatics and Presupposition', *Language*, 52 (1976) 1–17.

Katz, Jerrold J., and Paul M. Postal, *An Integrated Theory of Linguistic Descriptions* (Cambridge, Mass.: MIT Press, 1964).

Kermode, Frank, *Romantic Image* (New York: Random House, Vintage Books, 1964).

Klima, Edward S., 'Negation in English', in *The Structure of Language*, ed. J. A. Fodor and J. J. Katz (Englewood Cliffs, New Jersey: Prentice-Hall, 1964).

Klossowski, Pierre, 'Oubli et anamnèse dans l'expérience vécue de l'éternel retour du Même', in *Nietzsche*, Cahiers de Royaumont, Philosophie, no. VI (Paris: Minuit, 1967).

Kripke, Saul, *Naming and Necessity* (Cambridge, Mass.: Harvard University Press, 1980).

Kristeva, Julia, *La révolution du langage poétique: l'avant-garde à la fin du XIXe siècle: Lautréamont et Mallarmé* (Paris: Seuil, 1974).

——, 'Sémanalyse et production de sens: quelques problèmes de sémiotique littéraire à propos d'un texte de Mallarmé: *Un coup de dés*', in *Essais de sémiotique poétique*, ed. A. Greimas (Paris: Larousse, 1972).

——, *Séméiotikè: recherches pour une sémanalyse* (Paris: Seuil, 1969).

Kuroda, S.-Y., 'English Relativization and Certain Related Problems', in *Modern Studies in English*, ed. D. Reibel and S. Schane (Englewood Cliffs, New Jersey: Prentice-Hall, 1969).

Lacan, Jacques, *Ecrits* (Paris: Seuil, 1965).

——, 'La science et la vérité'. *Cahiers pour l'analyse*, nos. 1 and 2 (1966) 7–30.

——, *Le séminaire: Livre XI: Les quatre concepts fondamentaux de la psychanalyse* (Paris: Seuil, 1973).

Lacoue-Labarthe, Philippe, 'La dissimulation: Nietzsche, la question de l'art et la "littérature"', in *Nietzsche aujourd'hui?*, vol. 2 (Paris: Union Générale d'Editions, '10/18', 1973); repr. in *Le sujet de la philosophie* (Paris: Aubier-Flammarion, 1979).

——, *Le sujet de la philosophie* (Paris: Aubier-Flammarion, 1979).

——, 'Typographie', in *Mimesis des articulations*, by S. Agacinski, *et al.* (Paris: Aubier-Flammarion, 1975).

——, and Jean-Luc Nancy, eds, *L'absolu littéraire: théorie de la littérature du romantisme allemand* (Paris: Seuil, 1978).

Lakoff, George, 'Deep and Surface Grammar', mimeograph (Bloomington, Indiana: Indiana University Linguistics Club, 1968).

——, 'Global Rules', *Language*, 46 (1970) 627–39.

——, *Irregularity in Syntax* (New York: Holt, Rinehart & Winston, 1970).

——, 'On Generative Semantics', mimeograph (Bloomington, Indiana: Indiana University Linguistics Club, n.d.); repr. in *Semantics*, ed. D. D. Steinberg and L. A. Jakobovits (Cambridge: Cambridge University Press, 1971).

——, 'Pronouns and Reference', mimeograph (Bloomington, Indiana: Indiana University Linguistics Club, 1968).

——, and John R. Ross. 'Is Deep Structure Necessary?', mimeo-

graph (Bloomington, Indiana: Indiana University Linguistics Club, 1968).
Lakoff, Robin, 'Tense and Its Relation to Participants', *Language*, 46 (1970) 838–49.
Langbaum, Robert, 'The Exteriority of Self in Yeats's Poetry and Thought', *New Literary History*, 7 (1976) 579–97.
Lecointre, S., and J. Le Galliot, 'Le je(u) de l'énonciation', *Langages*, no. 31 (1973) 64–79.
Lees, Robert B., *The Grammar of English Nominalizations*, 5th printing (The Hague: Mouton, 1968).
Linsky, Leonard, *Names and Descriptions* (Chicago: University of Chicago Press, 1977).
——, *Referring* (London: Routledge & Kegan Paul, 1967).
Lyotard, Jean-François, *Discours, figure* (Paris: Klincksieck, 1971).
Mallarmé, Stéphane, *Oeuvres complètes*, ed. H. Mondor and G. Jean-Aubry (Paris: Gallimard, Bibliothèque de la Pléiade, 1945).
McCawley, James D., 'English as a VSO Language', *Language*, 46 (1970) 286–99.
——, 'The Role of Semantics in Grammar', in *Universals in Linguistic Theory*, ed. E. Bach and R. T. Harms (New York: Holt, Rinehart & Winston, 1968).
——, 'Where Do Noun Phrases Come From?', in *Readings in English Transformational Grammar*, ed. R. A. Jacobs and P. S. Rosenbaum (Waltham, Mass.: Ginn, 1970).
Miller, Jacques-Alain, 'La suture (éléments de la logique du significant)', *Cahiers pour l'analyse*, nos. 1 and 2 (1966) 39–51.
Miller, J. Hillis, *Poets of Reality: Six Twentieth-Century Writers* (Cambridge, Mass.: Harvard University Press, 1966).
Milner, Jean-Claude, 'Le point du signifiant', *Cahiers pour l'analyse*, no. 3 (1966) 73–82.
Montague, Richard, 'English as a Formal Language', in *Linguaggi nella società e nella tecnica*, by B. Visentini, *et al.* (Milan: Edizioni di Comunità, 1970); repr. in *Formal Philosophy: Selected Papers of Richard Montague*, ed. R. H. Thomason (New Haven: Yale University Press, 1974).
——, 'The Proper Treatment of Quantification in Ordinary English', in *Approaches to Natural Language*, ed. J. Hintikka *et al.* (Dordrecht: Reidel, 1973); repr. in *Formal Philosophy: Selected Papers of Richard Montague*, ed. R. H. Thomason (New Haven: Yale University Press, 1974).
Moore, Virginia, *The Unicorn: William Butler Yeats's Search for Reality*

(New York: Macmillan, 1954).
Nietzsche, Friedrich, 'Rhétorique et langage', texts translated, presented and annotated by P. Lacoue-Labarthe and J.-L. Nancy, *Poétique*, no. 5 (1971) 99–142.
——, *The Will to Power*, trans. W. Kaufman and R. J. Hollingdale; ed. W. Kaufman (New York: Random House, 1967).
Parkinson, Thomas, *W. B. Yeats: The Later Poetry* (Berkeley and Los Angeles: University of California Press, 1966).
Pierssens, Michel, *La tour de Babil: la fiction du signe* (Paris: Minuit, 1976).
Plato, *Cratylus, Parmenides, Greater Hippias, Lesser Hippias*, trans. H. N. Fowler (London: Heinemann, Loeb Classical Library, 1926).
——, *Theaetetus, Sophist*, trans. H. N. Fowler (London: Heinemann, Loeb Classical Library, 1921).
Plotinus, *The Enneads*, trans. S. MacKenna, 4th edn; rev. B. S. Page (New York: Pantheon, 1969).
Postal, Paul M., 'On Certain Ambiguities', *Linguistic Inquiry*, 5 (1974) 367–424.
——, 'On Coreferential Complement Subject Deletion', *Linguistic Inquiry*, 1 (1970) 439–500.
Quine, Willard V. O., *From a Logical Point of View*, 2nd edn (New York: Harper & Row, Harper Torchbooks, 1963).
——, *Word and Object* (Cambridge, Mass.: MIT Press, 1960).
Quirk, Randolph, 'Relative Clauses in Educated Spoken English', *English Studies*, 38 (1957) 97–109.
——, and Sidney Greenbaum, *A Concise Grammar of Contemporary English* (New York: Harcourt Brace Jovanovich, 1973).
Read, Herbert, *Phases of English Poetry* (Norfolk, Connecticut: New Directions, 1951).
Reibel, D., and S. Schane, eds, *Modern Studies in English: Readings in Transformational Grammar* (Englewood Cliffs, New Jersey: Prentice-Hall, 1969).
Roberts, Paul, *English Syntax* (New York: Harcourt Brace and World, 1964).
Rodman, Robert, 'Scope Phenomena, "Movement Transformations", and Relative Clauses', in *Montague Grammar*, ed. B. H. Partee (New York: Academic Press, 1976).
Rosenbaum, Peter S., *The Grammar of English Predicate Complement Constructions* (Cambridge, Mass.: MIT Press, 1967).
Ross, John R., 'Constraints on Variables in Syntax', Ph.D. dissertation, MIT, 1967.

Ross, John R., 'On Declarative Sentences', in *Readings in English Transformational Grammar*, ed. R. A. Jacobs and P. S. Rosenbaum (Waltham, Mass.: Ginn, 1970).

——, 'On the Cyclic Nature of English Pronominalization', in *To Honor Roman Jakobson* (The Hague: Mouton, 1967); repr. in *Modern Studies in English*, ed. D. Reibel and S. Schane (Englewood Cliffs, New Jersey: Prentice-Hall, 1969).

Russell, Bertrand, *Introduction to Mathematical Philosophy* (London: George Allen & Unwin, 1919).

——, *Logic and Knowledge: Essays 1901–1950*, ed. R. C. Marsh (London: George Allen & Unwin, 1956).

Rutherford, William E., 'Some Observations Concerning Subordinate Clauses in English', *Language*, 46 (1970) 97–115.

Ryle, Gilbert, 'Systematically Misleading Expressions', *Proceedings of the Aristotelian Society*, 1931–1932; repr. in *Logic and Language* (First and Second Series), ed. A. Flew (New York: Doubleday, Anchor Books, 1965).

Said, Edward W., *Beginnings: Intention and Method* (New York: Basic Books, 1975).

——, 'The Problem of Textuality: Two Exemplary Positions', *Critical Inquiry*, 4 (1978) 673–714.

Saussure, Ferdinand de, *Cours de linguistique générale*, ed. C. Bally and A. Sechehaye, with collaboration of A. Riedlinger, 3rd edn (Paris: Payot, 1931).

Schiller, Friedrich, *Essays Aesthetical and Philosophical* (London: George Bell & Sons, 1875).

Sebeok, Thomas A., ed., *Current Trends in Linguistics*: vol. 3: *Theoretical Foundations* (The Hague: Mouton, 1966).

Serres, Michel, *Hermès I: La communication* (Paris: Minuit, 1968).

——, *Hermès II: L'interférence* (Paris: Minuit, 1972).

——, *Hermès III: La traduction* (Paris: Minuit, 1974).

——, *Hermès IV: La distribution* (Paris: Minuit, 1977).

——, *Hermès V: Le passage du nord-ouest* (Paris: Minuit, 1980).

Smith, Carlota S., 'A Class of Complex Modifiers in English', *Language*, 37 (1961) 342–65.

——, 'Determiners and Relative Clauses in a Generative Grammar of English', *Language*, 40 (1964) 37–52.

Sollers, Philippe, *Logiques* (Paris: Seuil, 1968).

Sommerstein, Alan H., 'On the So-Called Definite Article in English', *Linguistic Inquiry*, 3 (1972) 197–209.

Spitzer, Leo, *Linguistics and Literary History: Essays in Stylistics*

(Princeton: Princeton University Press, 1948).
——, 'On Yeats's Poem "Leda and the Swan"', *Modern Philology*, 51 (1954) 271–6.
Stallworthy, Jon, *Between the Lines: Yeats's Poetry in the Making*, 2nd edn, with corrections (Oxford: Oxford University Press, 1965).
——, *Vision and Revision in Yeats's 'Last Poems'* (Oxford: Oxford University Press, 1969).
Steinberg, Danny D., and Leon A. Jakobovits, eds, *Semantics: An Interdisciplinary Reader in Philosophy, Linguistics and Psychology* (Cambridge: Cambridge University Press, 1971).
Strang, Barbara M. H., *Modern English Structure*, 2nd edn (London: Edward Arnold, 1968).
Strawson, P. F., *Individuals: an Essay in Descriptive Metaphysics* (London: Methuen, 1959).
Théorie d'ensemble (Paris: Seuil, 1968).
Thorne, J. P., 'On Nonrestrictive Relative Clauses', *Linguistic Inquiry*, 3 (1972) 552–6.
Todorov, Tzvetan, 'Problèmes de l'énonciation', *Langages*, no. 17 (1970) 3–11.
——, *Théories du symbole* (Paris: Seuil, 1977).
Trilling, Lionel, *Sincerity and Authenticity* (Cambridge, Mass.: Harvard University Press, 1972).
Unterecker, John, *A Reader's Guide to William Butler Yeats* (New York: Noonday, 1959).
Vaihinger, Hans, *The Philosophy of 'As if'*, trans. C. K. Ogden (London: Routledge & Kegan Paul, 1935).
Valéry, Paul, *Oeuvres*, ed. J. Hytier, 2 vols. (Paris: Gallimard, Bibliothèque de la Pléiade, 1957).
Veeder, William R., *W. B. Yeats: The Rhetoric of Repetition* (Berkeley and Los Angeles: University of California Press, 1968).
Wasow, Thomas, 'Anaphoric Pronouns and Bound Variables', *Language*, 51 (1975) 368–83.
Weinrich, Harald, *Le temps*, trans. M. Lacoste (Paris: Seuil, 1973).
Werth, Paul, 'Some Thoughts on Non-Restrictive Relatives', *Linguistics*, no. 142 (1974) 33–67.
Whitaker, Thomas R., 'W. B. Yeats: History and the Shaping Joy', in *Edwardians and Late Victorians*, ed. R. Ellmann (New York: Columbia University Press, 1960).
Wilde, Oscar, *The Works of Oscar Wilde* (New York: Lamb Publishing Co., 1909).

Wilson, F. A. C., *W. B. Yeats and Tradition* (London: Methuen, 1958).
Wittgenstein, Ludwig, *Philosophical Investigations*, trans. G. E. M. Anscombe, 2nd edn (New York: Macmillan, 1958).
Yeats, William Butler, *The Autobiography of William Butler Yeats* (New York: Macmillan, 1953).
——, *Essays and Introductions* (New York: Macmillan, 1961).
——, *Explorations* (New York: Macmillan, 1962).
——, *The Letters of W. B. Yeats*, ed. A. Wade (New York: Macmillan, 1955).
——, *Mythologies* (New York: Macmillan, 1959).
——, *The Variorum Edition of the Plays of W. B. Yeats*, ed. R. K. Alspach (New York: Macmillan, 1966).
——, *The Variorum Edition of the Poems of W. B. Yeats*, ed. P. Allt and R. K. Alspach, 4th printing (New York: Macmillan, 1968).
——, *A Vision* (New York: Macmillan, 1956).
——, *W. B. Yeats and T. Sturge Moore: Their Correspondence 1901–1937*, ed. U. Bridge (New York: Oxford University Press, 1953).
Ziff, Paul, *Semantic Analysis* (Ithaca: Cornell University Press, 1960).

Glossary

allocutor: The person to whom a discourse is addressed. Considered one of the participants in the discourse. If the discourse is spoken, the allocutor is the hearer. In grammatical terms, the allocutor is the referent of the pronoun *you*.

anaphoric: Referring back to a previous occurrence of the same item or its equivalent. The term is applied to a use of the definite determiners. The anaphoric use of a determiner marks a noun phrase as fully identified in the context of a previous mention or occurrence of the noun phrase.

cataphoric: Referring forward. The term is applied to a use of the definite determiners. The cataphoric use of a determiner marks a noun phrase as fully identified when there is a potentially defining modifier within the noun phrase and in the absence of a previous occurrence (actual or implied) of the noun phrase.

count noun: A noun referring to an entity that can be counted, such as *tree*. A count noun may occur with any of the determiners.

determiner: One of a class of words, including the articles, which have the same potential positions in the noun phrase as the articles, and which serve to limit the reference of the following noun. (In the present study, such quantifying words as *all, some, much, every*, etc. are not considered determiners.) The determiners signal whether or not the following noun requires identification, and, if so, whether or not that identification is to be considered complete. The claim of complete identification is effected by the definite determiners, which include *the*, the demonstratives (*that, those, this,* and *these*), and the possessives (*his, her*, etc.). The claim of incomplete identification is effected by the indefinite determiners. These include the singular indefinite determiner *a* (*an*) and the plural indefinite determiner, the form of which is null, i.e., the absence of any explicit determining word.

Glossary

discourse situation: The specific setting, primarily the physical surroundings, within which a discourse takes place. When a noun phrase is identified by means of direct reference to a feature of the discourse situation, the identification is said to be effected by the 'situational' use of the noun's determiner. (See *situational*.)

information unit: A segment of speech set off as a discrete part of the total message. The segmentation of the message is effected by pauses. Though any part of the message may be thus defined as a unit, the most usual unit is the clause. An example is the non-restrictive relative clause. The pauses setting it off as a segment are represented in the written language by commas.

locutor: The person producing a discourse. If the discourse is spoken, the locutor is the speaker. In grammatical terms, the locutor is the referent of the pronoun *I*.

noncount noun: A noun referring to an entity which cannot be counted, such as *air* or *imagination*. Noncount nouns take the null determiner. If pluralised or if used with the singular indefinite determiner *a* (*an*), a noncount noun will be interpreted as a count noun.

noun phrase: Any word or group of words which functions like a noun in a sentence (the usual functions being subject, object, or complement). The most frequent noun phrases consist of common nouns (plus their adjuncts), proper nouns, or pronouns. In the case of common nouns, the noun phrase will include the noun itself, its determiner, and sometimes a quantifier (such as *all* or *every*) and one or more modifiers.

null determiner (or **null**): The determiner signalled by the absence of any determining word before the noun. In normal use, the null determiner has two main functions: it accompanies noncount nouns (e.g., 'Pour wine'); and it signals incomplete identification for a plural count noun, marking the noun as indefinite (e.g., 'Crowds gathered').

presuppositional: A term describing the operation of all those definite determiners which effect identification by reference to pre-established or presupposed knowledge shared by locutor and allocutor. In characterising the modes of identification effected by determiners, 'presuppositional' is a broader term than 'anaphoric', 'cataphoric' or 'situational', for 'presuppositional' describes the anaphoric use of *the* and the demonstratives as well as the situational use of *the*.

situational: A use of the definite determiners whereby they effect the identification of a noun phrase by means of direct reference to a feature of the discourse situation. A situational reference is thus non-textual, while anaphoric and cataphoric references are textual. (See *discourse situation*.)

Index

additive structuring, 56–71
adjective, 11, 27–42, 48, 89n.1, 90–1n.2, 92n.12
allocutor, 13, 17, 21, 80–1, 89n.2, *see also* locutor
anaphoric, *see* determiner, anaphoric use of
Anglo-Irish, 87–8n.10
antiplatonism, 1, 3, 7, 10–12, 82, 87n.2, n.7
Austin, J. L., 94n.11

Barthes, Roland, 87n.1
Benveniste, Emile, 89n.21, 94n.2
Bergson, Henri, 88n.13

cataphoric, *see* determiner, cataphoric use of
contraction, 9–11, 17, 23–5, 88n.13, n.16
Coleridge, S. T., 11, 88n.16
count and noncount nouns, 36–40, 54, 93n.13

Deleuze, Gilles, 7–11, 23, 87n.1–2, n.7, 88n.12–13, 94n.1
demonstrative, *see* determiner, demonstrative
Derrida, Jacques, 87n.1
Descartes, René, 87n.2
determiner, 13–27, 45–7, 74, 78, 89n.1, 89–90n.4
  anaphoric use of, 14–28, 30–8, 45, 47, 90n.6, n.8, 91n.4–5, n.7, 94n.9
  cataphoric use of, 28–36, 41, 47, 77, 90n.8, 91n.6, 94n.9
  demonstrative, 11, 13–27, 31–2, 47, 80, 89n.3, 89–90n.4, 90n.5–6, n.8, 91n.6

'null', 13–14, 28, 36–41, 53, 55, 89–90n.4, 92n.12
'presuppositional' uses of, 13, 15–26, 32
situational use of, 14–26, 80, 90n.5, n.7–8, 91n.6, 94n.9
the, 13–21, 24, 27–35, 38, 47, 89–90n.4, 90n.5, 91n.4
difference, 1, 4–13, 15, 17–18, 23, 25–7, 48, 55–6, 58, 64–5, 68, 72–3, 79, 82, 87n.1–2, 88n.17, 94n.1
Diver, William, 94n.2, n.4

Eliot, T. S., 12

Foucault, Michel, 87n.1–2, 89n.20

Gaelic, 87–8n.10
Gregory, Lady Augusta, 87–8n.10
gyres, 11, 34

Halliday, M. A. K., 14, 28, 30, 34, 44, 59, 90n.5, n.8, n.1, 91n.4, n.6–7, 92n.3–4, n.6, 93n.3, 94n.8–9
Hegel, G. W. F., 87n.2

information unit, 44–50, 52, 56–7, 59–60, 62, 67, 92n.6
intonation contour, 44, 49–51, 92n.6

Jacobs, Roderick, 89n.3, 92n.1, 93n.4
Jakobson, Roman, 3, 87n.6
Joyce, James, 12

Kant, Immanuel, 87n.2
Kirsner, Robert, 93n.13
Kristeva, Julia, 36, 87n.1, 92n.10

Index

locutor, 17, 19, 79–81, 89n.2, *see also* allocutor

Mallarmé, Stéphane, 88n.17
modernism, 11–12, 88–9n.17

Nietzsche, Friedrich, 12
noncount nouns, *see* count and noncount nouns
'null', *see* determiner, 'null'

paradigm, 4, 6, 10, 15, 25, 65, 73
Parkinson, Thomas, 92n.12
platonism, 1–3, 7, 10–11, 72, 89n.21
polysyndeton, 65–8, *see also* additive structuring
post-structuralism, 3, 7, 87n.1
presuppositional, *see* determiner, 'presuppositional' uses of
Proust, Marcel, 12

Quirk, Randolph, 87–8n.10, 92n.2, n.7

relative clause, 4–6, 10, 42–58, 60, 63, 70, 78, 89n.1, 90n.9, 90–1n.2, 91n.3, n.5, 92n.1–2, 93n.12, n.1, n.5–6
relative pronoun, 5–6, 42, 51–3, 87–8n.10, 92n.9–11 (*Chapter 3*)
repetition, 7–11, 72, 82
Roberts, Paul, 89–90n.4
romanticism, 11, 88n.16, 89n.19
Rosenbaum, Peter, 89n.3, 91n.7, 92n.1, 93n.4

Saussure, Ferdinand de, 6–7, 88n.11
Schiller, Friedrich, 89n.19
semiotics, 2
series, 8–11, 15, 17, 23, 55–6, 64, 72–3, 82, 94n.1
situational, *see* determiner, situational use of
Smith, Carlota, 91n.3
Sollers, Philippe, 87n.1
Spitzer, Leo, 2, 87n.4–5
Stallworthy, Jon, 92n.5
Strang, Barbara, 87n.3
structuralism, 2–3

stylistics, 2
subject, 1–3, 7, 9–12, 17, 24–6, 31–6, 60, 87n.2, 88n.13, 89n.21

tense, 2, 28, 72–82, 94n.2–7, n.9–11 (*Chapter 5*)
the, *see* determiner, *the*
time, 2, 72–82, 94n.1, n.11
Todorov, Tzvetan, 89n.2
Trilling, Lionel, 89n.18–19

Unterecker, John, 91n.8

Wilde, Oscar, 12, 89n.19
Wordsworth, William, 92.n.11

Yeats, William Butler
'Among School Children', 16, 52–5
Autobiography, 88–9n.17
'The Ballad of Father O'Hart', 45
'Blood and the Moon', 90n.7
'Byzantium', 24, 34, 90n.10
'The Circus Animals' Desertion', 33
'Cuchulain's Fight with the Sea', 20
'Death', 28
'A Deep-sworn Vow', 20
'A Dialogue of Self and Soul', 90n.7
'Easter 1916', 34
'Ego Dominus Tuus', 90n.7
'The Fisherman', 62–4
'Her Anxiety', 64–5
'His Dream', 33
'In Memory of Major Report Gregory', 90n.7
'Leda and the Swan', 30, 34–6, 39–40, 91n.7–9
Letters, 92n.5
'Meditations in Time of Civil War', 90n.7
'Michael Robartes and the Dancer', 18
Mythologies, 88n.14
'News for the Delphic Oracle', 61–2
'The Phases of the Moon', 18, 90n.7

Index

additive structuring, 56–71
adjective, 11, 27–42, 48, 89n.1, 90–1n.2, 92n.12
allocutor, 13, 17, 21, 80–1, 89n.2, *see also* locutor
anaphoric, *see* determiner, anaphoric use of
Anglo-Irish, 87–8n.10
antiplatonism, 1, 3, 7, 10–12, 82, 87n.2, n.7
Austin, J. L., 94n.11

Barthes, Roland, 87n.1
Benveniste, Emile, 89n.21, 94n.2
Bergson, Henri, 88n.13

cataphoric, *see* determiner, cataphoric use of
contraction, 9–11, 17, 23–5, 88n.13, n.16
Coleridge, S. T., 11, 88n.16
count and noncount nouns, 36–40, 54, 93n.13

Deleuze, Gilles, 7–11, 23, 87n.1–2, n.7, 88n.12–13, 94n.1
demonstrative, *see* determiner, demonstrative
Derrida, Jacques, 87n.1
Descartes, René, 87n.2
determiner, 13–27, 45–7, 74, 78, 89n.1, 89–90n.4
    anaphoric use of, 14–28, 30–8, 45, 47, 90n.6, n.8, 91n.4–5, n.7, 94n.9
    cataphoric use of, 28–36, 41, 47, 77, 90n.8, 91n.6, 94n.9
    demonstrative, 11, 13–27, 31–2, 47, 80, 89n.3, 89–90n.4, 90n.5–6, n.8, 91n.6

'null', 13–14, 28, 36–41, 53, 55, 89–90n.4, 92n.12
    'presuppositional' uses of, 13, 15–26, 32
    situational use of, 14–26, 80, 90n.5, n.7–8, 91n.6, 94n.9
    the, 13–21, 24, 27–35, 38, 47, 89–90n.4, 90n.5, 91n.4
difference, 1, 4–13, 15, 17–18, 23, 25–7, 48, 55–6, 58, 64–5, 68, 72–3, 79, 82, 87n.1–2, 88n.17, 94n.1
Diver, William, 94n.2, n.4

Eliot, T. S., 12

Foucault, Michel, 87n.1–2, 89n.20

Gaelic, 87–8n.10
Gregory, Lady Augusta, 87–8n.10
gyres, 11, 34

Halliday, M. A. K., 14, 28, 30, 34, 44, 59, 90n.5, n.8, n.1, 91n.4, n.6–7, 92n.3–4, n.6, 93n.3, 94n.8–9
Hegel, G. W. F., 87n.2

information unit, 44–50, 52, 56–7, 59–60, 62, 67, 92n.6
intonation contour, 44, 49–51, 92n.6

Jacobs, Roderick, 89n.3, 92n.1, 93n.4
Jakobson, Roman, 3, 87n.6
Joyce, James, 12

Kant, Immanuel, 87n.2
Kirsner, Robert, 93n.13
Kristeva, Julia, 36, 87n.1, 92n.10

locutor, 17, 19, 79–81, 89n.2, *see also* allocutor

Mallarmé, Stéphane, 88n.17
modernism, 11–12, 88–9n.17

Nietzsche, Friedrich, 12
noncount nouns, *see* count and noncount nouns
'null', *see* determiner, 'null'

paradigm, 4, 6, 10, 15, 25, 65, 73
Parkinson, Thomas, 92n.12
platonism, 1–3, 7, 10–11, 72, 89n.21
polysyndeton, 65–8, *see also* additive structuring
post-structuralism, 3, 7, 87n.1
presuppositional, *see* determiner, 'presuppositional' uses of
Proust, Marcel, 12

Quirk, Randolph, 87–8n.10, 92n.2, n.7

relative clause, 4–6, 10, 42–58, 60, 63, 70, 78, 89n.1, 90n.9, 90–1n.2, 91n.3, n.5, 92n.1–2, 93n.12, n.1, n.5–6
relative pronoun, 5–6, 42, 51–3, 87–8n.10, 92n.9–11 (*Chapter 3*)
repetition, 7–11, 72, 82
Roberts, Paul, 89–90n.4
romanticism, 11, 88n.16, 89n.19
Rosenbaum, Peter, 89n.3, 91n.7, 92n.1, 93n.4

Saussure, Ferdinand de, 6–7, 88n.11
Schiller, Friedrich, 89n.19
semiotics, 2
series, 8–11, 15, 17, 23, 55–6, 64, 72–3, 82, 94n.1
situational, *see* determiner, situational use of
Smith, Carlota, 91n.3
Sollers, Philippe, 87n.1
Spitzer, Leo, 2, 87n.4–5
Stallworthy, Jon, 92n.5
Strang, Barbara, 87n.3
structuralism, 2–3

stylistics, 2
subject, 1–3, 7, 9–12, 17, 24–6, 31–6, 60, 87n.2, 88n.13, 89n.21

tense, 2, 28, 72–82, 94n.2–7, n.9–11 (*Chapter 5*)
the, *see* determiner, *the*
time, 2, 72–82, 94n.1, n.11
Todorov, Tzvetan, 89n.2
Trilling, Lionel, 89n.18–19

Unterecker, John, 91n.8

Wilde, Oscar, 12, 89n.19
Wordsworth, William, 92.n.11

Yeats, William Butler
'Among School Children', 16, 52–5
Autobiography, 88–9n.17
'The Ballad of Father O'Hart', 45
'Blood and the Moon', 90n.7
'Byzantium', 24, 34, 90n.10
'The Circus Animals' Desertion', 33
'Cuchulain's Fight with the Sea', 20
'Death', 28
'A Deep-sworn Vow', 20
'A Dialogue of Self and Soul', 90n.7
'Easter 1916', 34
'Ego Dominus Tuus', 90n.7
'The Fisherman', 62–4
'Her Anxiety', 64–5
'His Dream', 33
'In Memory of Major Report Gregory', 90n.7
'Leda and the Swan', 30, 34–6, 39–40, 91n.7–9
Letters, 92n.5
'Meditations in Time of Civil War', 90n.7
'Michael Robartes and the Dancer', 18
Mythologies, 88n.14
'News for the Delphic Oracle', 61–2
'The Phases of the Moon', 18, 90n.7

Index

'A Prayer for my Daughter', 90n.7
'A Prayer on going into my House', 90n.7
'The Resurrection', 90n.6
'The Sad Shepherd', 91n.5
Sailing to Byzantium', 24
'The Second Coming', 34
'The Song of Wandering Aengus', 29
'The Statues', 29–30
'Symbols', 14
'To be carved on a stone at Thoor Ballylee', 19, 90n.7

The Tower, 90n.7
'The Tower', 46, 90n.7
'Two Songs from a Play', 34, 90n.6
Variorum Edition of the Plays, 87–8n.10
Variorum Edition of the Poems, 83, 87n.9, 91n.5
A Vision, 11, 88n.15
'While I, from that reed-throated whisperer', 70–1, 94n.9–10
The Wild Swans at Coole, 90n.7
'The Wild Swans at Coole', 33

To Ireland in the Coming Times.

Know that I would accounted be
True brother of that company
Who sang to sweeten Ireland's wrong
Ballad and story, rann and song